Blatant Christianity

Living
By the Sermon on the Mount

By J. E. Becker

Landmark Press, GA

Blatant Christianity Living by the Sermon on the Mount
Copyright© 2013 By J. E. Becker all rights reserved to free use in the Kingdom of God.
Published by Landmark Press, 1800 Liberty Grove Road,
 Alpharetta, GA 30004
To see other books by J. E. Becker go to website www.jebecker.com
Scripture quotes are from The Authorized Version, ASV, Other "Scripture taken from the New King James Version®. Copyright © 1982 by Thomas Nelson, Inc. Used by permission. All rights reserved."

          Published in the United States of America
          ISBN 978-0-9617493-1-6
          Life Changing Christian Living

Acknowledgments

I would be completely remiss if I did not acknowledge the debt I owe to three great teachers from whom I have distilled the teaching in this book. For the teaching on body, soul and spirit I owe Watchman Knee for his 3 volume set, *The Spiritual Man,* Bill Gothard for the teachings in his Basic Youth Conflicts seminars and Bob Mumford for his classification and naming of most of the laws taught in his tapes on the Sermon on the Mount. As to the manuscript, I am deeply indebted to Linda Muzunik for hunting down recalcitrant commas, and other grammar insufficiencies. My son Adam Becker is greatly appreciated for helping with computer emergencies and for reading through the final proof.

Table of Contents

Introduction..7

   Section One: Salvation Basics

Chapter 1 The Soul...13
Chapter 2 The Spirit Gives Life—Plus........................35
Chapter 3 Made in His Image......................................63

   Section Two: Attitudes and Laws

Chapter 4 Attitudes: Plus the Laws............................79

   Section Three: The Laws

Chapter 5   The Law of Anger.......................................95
Chapter 6 The Law of Purity....................................111
Chapter 7 The Law of Fidelity..................................121
Chapter 8 The Law of Flexiblity................................129
Chapter 9 The Law of Impartiality...........................137
Chapter 10 The Law of Devotion..............................147
Chapter 11 The Law of Acquisition..........................165
Chapter 12 The Law of Criticism..............................173
Chapter 13 The Law of Understanding....................181

   Section : Robbers

Chapter 14 Fruit Robbers..207

   Section Five: Rewarding Works

Chapter 15 Rewarding the Unworthy............................231
Chapter 16 Rewarding the Worthy.................................251

Introduction

When I was a young Christian trying to walk in God's ways, I took my next-door neighbor to an evangelistic meeting at our church. She raised her hand when the evangelist asked if anyone wanted to become a Christian. As the evangelist began to question her to see how much she understood, she pointed to me and said, "I just want to be like her." I did not even know what I did to impress her. Of course, it was not I who impressed her, but Christ, living in me.

We are like my neighbor. If we see the excellence of Jesus, we want to be like him. To be like him we need a full complement of the fruits of the Spirit, because Jesus revealed the nature of the Father to the world in the same way. Yet, we are not told exactly how to acquire these venerable traits. Instead, Paul contrasts the fruits of the Spirit to traits of the flesh. Then, after naming the fruits of the Spirit, he admonishes, "If we live in the Spirit, let us also walk in the Spirit" (Gal.5:25). Thus, it seems that walking in the Spirit will somehow produce the Spirit's fruit. Again, specifically, how do we do this? Jesus gave us a clue when he spoke to his disciples by saying:

> A little while longer and the world will see Me no more, but you will see Me. Because I live, you will live also.
>
> At that day you will know that I am in My Father, and you in Me, and I in you. He who has My commandments and keeps them, it is he who loves Me. And

he who loves Me will be loved by My Father, and I will love him and manifest Myself to him.

Judas (not Iscariot) said to Him, "Lord, how is it that You will manifest Yourself to us, and not to the world?"

Jesus answered and said to him, "If anyone loves Me, he will keep My word; and My Father will love him, and We will come to him and make Our home with him.

He who does not love Me does not keep My words; and the word which you hear is not Mine but the Father's who sent Me.

John 14:19-24 NKJV

Just what are these commandments? I would like to suggest that the most organized form of commandments found in a complete set are those written in Matthew's account of the Sermon on the Mount. Actually, Jesus seemed to repeat these instructions over and over again all through the gospels. The only other direct commandments that I know of are the commandment to disciples (1) to love one another, and (2) to watch for his coming. These are universal; however, the commandments in the Sermon on the Mount tell us how to live.

For three years Jesus taught his disciples and the people of Israel along one theme—the kingdom of God. Under that theme, he went beyond the Old Testament law by saying, "I came not to destroy the law . . . but to fulfill it" (Matthew 5:17). God gave the Old Testament law to expose sin. By contrast, the commandments Jesus gave were to govern and to develop righteousness. The Holy Spirit, living in the hearts of believers, enables them to live a higher standard of righteousness than the people before Christ came. Therefore, if we obey Jesus' commandments, we can develop personal righteousness in the kingdom of God through the Holy Spirit. It makes sense that if we live in subject to a king, we have to obey the laws he makes. Therefore, I call the commandments in the Sermon on the Mount the laws of the kingdom.

Although these laws written in Matthew 5, 6 and 7 seem to be several, I discovered that the individual laws could to be reduced to nine, some with more than one part. If that were true, it probably meant that each law could be matched to a single beatitude. Then I discovered a wondrous thing. If we pose the right attitude when we obey the corresponding law, we automatically produce one of the nine fruits of the Spirit. Could this be the reason the Holy Spirit prefaced the laws with the beatitudes?

However, Jesus was not talking about a set of rules we *must do* when He called His teachings commandments. They are not like the laws the Jews developed into a legalistic system. These new laws resemble the laws of nature. If we throw an apple up into the air, it will come down, according to the law of gravity. In the same manner, if we have a correct attitude toward the area of life targeted where we are prone to sin, and act according to its particular law of righteousness, a fruit of the Spirit begins to develop automatically. If the commandment is continually obeyed, full ripened fruit develops over a period of time. At this point of in the soul's development, Jesus and his Father can alive inside the person full of such fruits, showing themselves to the world!

The Old Testament Laws, if broken, brought condemnations and punishment, because they targeted sin. In contrast, these New Testament Laws, *if kept*, bring blessings and rewards, because they show us how to overcome sin. I was teaching a class of teenagers in Sunday School at the time when I discovered this. The lessons so inspired my students that some took their notes with them to college as a pattern to live by.

But, before we take up the individual laws, we need to understand the words and terms used in the Scripture that relate to salvation and the kingdom of God. Clarifying these basics of Christianity enables us to understand the whole purpose of God's dealings with men.

What does the Bible mean when it speaks of our "heart," our "soul," or our "spirit"? If we do not understand the Biblical terms, we will miss the "why" behind much of the instruction on righteous living. Therefore, before we attempt to learn the laws, we will try to define "religious words" that even mature Christians may have become "too accustomed to" that their importance is lost. Specifically, we will define the words "soul" and "spirit," and identify their functions. Then we will compare the same functions to God, and how He works. After we see God's purpose unfold, as He designed in the Scripture, we will look at the laws designed to make us like Him.

SECTION ONE
Salvation Basics

1

The Soul

When Mary, the mother of our Lord, approached her cousin, Elizabeth, she said, "My soul doth magnify the Lord, and my spirit hath rejoiced in God my Saviour" (Luke 1:46, 47). In this simple statement, Mary distinguished her soul from her spirit. Her soul exalted the Lord in his greatness, while her spirit reveled in the joy of His goodness to her.

Paul the apostle goes a step further. saying to the Thessalonians, "And the very God of peace sanctify you wholly; and I pray God your *whole spirit and soul and body* be preserved blameless unto the coming of our Lord Jesus Christ" (1 Thessalonians. 5:23 AV - Emphasis mine). So, according to Paul, the soul is not only separate from the spirit, but also from the body. In other words, the soul forms a unique entity, being one third of the whole person.

When God created Adam, the Bible says, "And the Lord God formed man of the dust of the ground [the elements], speaking of his physical body, He breathed into his nostrils the breath of life [spirit]; and man became a living soul" (Gen. 2:7). From this Scripture we might deduce that the soul initially formed by the infusing of life (vitality) into the physical elements (the dust of the earth). The life came from God. That's why evolution won't work. The physical elements alone can never begin life.

However, God divided Adam's life into two lives when he made Eve. Henceforth, all souls will be made by combining the life from two souls who have become one by marriage. Thus, life comes from already existing life, and the new soul born from two parent's combines elements from both to create an entirely unique person, different from the parents.

A sperm, or seed as the Bible calls it, carries half the chromosomes to form the DNA needed to build a new body. The other twenty-four are in the female egg. When the sperm/seed combines with the female egg, life (vitality) begins a new soul. The cells immediately begin to divide and grow to form a body. If all life begins, as did Adam's, by the infusion of vitality into the uniquely combined physical elements, then we can expect that all souls begin at conception.

Life, transferred from the father's sperm, to add the life in the mother's egg, forms a combined cell called a zygote. At first, all life sustaining power comes from the mother, who nourishes the fetus. But eventually the fetus's own blood develops and begins to nourish its tiny body. Each step of its growth develops another stage toward independence, all according to the vitality written in the DNA, which contains the pattern for its development. Eventually, again because of its unique makeup, its tiny soul begins to respond to outside stimuli.

Circumstances and experiment, both, tend to confirm that the soul forms before birth. According to studies conducted in the nineties, and reported in Psychology Today

(Sept/Oct 1998), a fetus of thirty-two weeks acts no different than a birth baby (thirty-six weeks).

The experts found that the fetus responds to external physical factors such as light and sound. They can distinguish the voice of their mother from a stranger. They even enjoy being read to, reacting more favorably to often read stories as opposed to others. Other studies show that the emotions, and stresses, of the mother, also affect the fetus. Janet DiPietro, of Johns Hopkins University found that mothers who work in heavy, stress-filled jobs (especially in the last trimester), have highly active fetuses, and give birth to irritable babies.

Some mothers opting for a contented baby, sing to their unborn babies or read stories to them from the seventh month on, since this is when a baby first hears. Sometimes even the fathers get involved.

Besides the clinical studies, two incidents in Scripture also seem to confirm that the soul is formed before birth. Jacob and Esau wrestled within Rebekah's womb so much, that she questioned God about it. His answer indicated that strong, contrasting, personalities were already forming; personalities that later would form nations, that hated each other (Genesis 25:2, 23).

The New Testament reports that the soul of John the Baptist leaped for joy in Elizabeth's womb, in response to the voice of his Lord's mother (Luke 1:44). Even today, every mother knows that each of her babies has its distinctive [soul] personality from birth. How could this be true unless the soul was developing at the same time as the body?

The Definition of the Soul

Now let's check the Scriptures to further break down and define how the Bible uses the term "the soul." Using the Englishman's Concordance division in computer Bible software, I traced "nephesh," the Hebrew word for soul through the Old Testament, to see how it was translated into English. Besides all the references simply translated "soul," in twelve references "nephesh" was translated "mind"; in eight references it was translated "will" or "desire"; in thirteen references it was translated into various emotions such as "angry," "discontented," "pleasure," and "love." I concluded that this must be why teachers define the soul as the mind, the will, and the emotions of an individual.

New Testament definition of soul continues along the same line. The Greek word for soul "psyche" translates into "life," "lives," and "heart" as well as "mind" and the emotion filled word, "heartily." Perhaps the most significant word here is "heart. In religious circles we speak of the heart as troubled, defiled, heavy, sinful, and desperately needing change.

Although the Authorized Version uses the Greek word psyche" for "heart" in two places, "kardia" is the usual Greek word translated heart. Strong's Concordance gives the following definition: "kardia, prolonged from a primary kar (Latin, cor, "heart"); the heart, i.e. (figuratively) the thoughts (mind) or feelings (emotions); also (by analogy) the very center of the soul," apparently derived from the soul's thoughts and feelings. This may be the reason the Scriptures use a separate word for heart. It is more than mind, will and emotions. The heart is like a receptacle that saves the combined attitudes of the spirit, with past actions of the soul, and stores them in the brain as a pool of opinions formulating the man's unique attitudes, desires, likes, dislikes, goals, faith, even his moral standard. For even Jesus said all defilement comes from the heart (Matthew 15:19, 20 AV).

Dr. Caroline Leaf, who has studied the physical brain for twenty-some years, can show where the different functions of the soul occupy the brain. In fact, she says the physical heart of the body has its own 40,000 neuron-cell, mini-brain, that acts like a conscience, telling the 200,000,000,000 (trillion)-neuron cell brain in the head, what things are good, or bad, for the body, affecting decisions. (See her book, Your Body, His Temple.)

This pool of opinions, which is constantly changing according to our latest opinion about a matter, motivates all of our actions accordingly. So, when the Bible speaks of the soul, it is a general term indicating a specific personality. When it speaks of a man's heart, it is particularly dealing with that pool of opinions and attitudes that he has accumulated inside, that make him uniquely "him." The "biblical heart," then, is the driving force behind the will and the center of the soul. Since the heart acts as the center of man, we can understand why God often refers to it instead of the soul. God reaches for the center of the center. Jesus said, "For out of the heart proceed evil thoughts, murders, adulteries, fornication, thefts, false witness, blasphemies. These are the things that defile a man . . . "(Matthew 15:19,20a). If God can get the heart right, the whole person will be right.

How the Soul Functions

Now that we understand the Scriptural meaning for soul and heart, let's look at how they function with the rest of the person: the body and the spirit.

Body, soul and spirit in reality function as totally integrated, and work together at lightning speed. Our separation of them is only for the purpose of learning and might be compared to a slow-motion video clip, seen as God views mankind.

Scripture often speaks of the soul, the spirit, or the heart, and occasionally, of the body. The body probes the natural material world with its five sensors: sight, sound, smell, taste, and touch. The soul, through the mind, acts as a clearinghouse for this information. Although the signals are registered in the brain, the brain probably does not "think." While the ability to reason lies wholly in the brain, the workings of it, the mind, probably runs over the nerve cells like fingers over a piano to produce music.

A computer illustrates this because of its electrical connections resemble human thinking. The brain, like all the rest of the body, can be compared to a piece of "hardware" containing all the "wiring." The mind directs the thought patterns across the "wiring," just as the signal from the keyboard of a computer operates the proper switches in the "motherboard" to execute the command. Also, like a computer connected to active peripherals such as a modem, microphone, or scanner, the body (hardware) gathers information by its probes. Information from the senses continually pours into the mind to be analyzed, sorted, and decided upon by the will. The mind and will, however, do not act on information alone.

The feelings of the emotions also contribute. Here the analogy to the computer breaks down, since a computer cannot feel. A man, however, has strong emotions that affect his decisions. He decides according to the facts known—providing the passions of the emotions don't interfere. Strong memories stored by the heart are charged with all kinds of emotions. Dr. Leaf shows slides of slices of the brain where strong negative memories appear as thick, thorny, bramble bushes in the brain. These negative memories cause the heart to send signals to the brain ordering it to produce toxic chemicals that can make the body sick. Bitter memories stored with strong emotions continue to poison the body as long as they are reviewed.

Because of, or despite, the influence of the mind and the emotions, the volition, or will of a person determines all action. A man's will decides where he will go, what he will do, what he will say, and even what he will believe. So, we would have to say that the soul containing the will, motivated by the heart that influences it, serves as the command center of the whole person.

On the other hand, the spirit of man is his vitality. Using the analogy of the computer again, if the body is the "hardware," then the spirit must be the electric power that turns it on and enables it to function. But as every computer owner knows, the computer can be turned on, the screen lit and power extending to every peripheral machine, but it will not function unless software has been loaded, and there is purposeful, intelligent input.

In the same way, a person in a coma has vitality but no apparent consciousness. Some failing in the brain imprisons his soul, so that it cannot direct the body. He has no command center, therefore no ability to feed or to perform all the things necessary to sustain life. If his body can be kept alive artificially by modern medicine, i.e. by IV's, breathing machines, etc., his spirit will maintain vitality. Nevertheless, a live body without a soul is called a vegetable.

During an accident, our son suffered a blood clot in the main artery to the brain. He lingered ten days on life support, in a coma, before ultimately succumbing. The cutting off of the blood supply to the brain shut down his consciousness, and eventually caused his brain to die. But meanwhile, as his body was on life support and his spirit still remained, his surface wounds began to heal. His spirit, his vitality, had begun rebuilding his body.

When there is a complete breakdown of vital function, the spirit leaves the body at death. Thus the spirit is the power pack that supplies the energy to move the body, to interface the soul to the brain, and to run the unconscious functions of the body, such as healing.

Another function of the spirit is communication. Just as the body communicates with the natural realm, the spirit communicates with the spiritual realm. Like the body, it too has diverse sensors. Whereas the body has five senses, the spirit has four: two to interact with the mind and two to interact with the emotions. (1) The first is creative imagination, which mimics God in creativity. (2) The second is intuition, the ability to receive knowledge from the spiritual realm completely apart from the natural perception of the body. These interact with the mind. (3) The third is conscience, which registers guilt for wrongdoing, and (4) the fourth is worship, which provides man with a strong drive to adore God (or a god). These two interact with the emotions. The soul receives input from these spiritual facilities and also directs all spiritual activity through the will.

Now let us look at how all these functions together. The body sends signals to the brain, where the mind assimilates the information of a situation. Then (according to College Psychology 101), the mind passes the information through the emotions (seated in the heart) to see if it is a threat to life or ego, or pleasant to life or ego.

If the mind perceives danger, fright or anger, the perception registers not only in the physical network, but also in the emotions, which causes the spirit to activate the Endocrine System. It releases adrenaline into the bloodstream. The heart pumps blood vigorously to the muscles, as the body prepares for flight or fight according to the choice of the will. The spirit generates phenomenal energy in answer to a threat.

If the mind perceives pleasure such as a beautiful sight, sound, smell, taste or touch, or a personal compliment from a friend praising his appearance or abilities, the emotions experience delight. Here the spirit is at rest and experiences peace.

But the spirit does more than just protect the species. When the creative imagination of the person becomes involved, he may desire [will] to capture the fleeting beauties of the natural world on canvas, stone, or film. Or he might design various patterns, buildings, or gardens. Maybe a more practical-minded individual would invent work-saving or communicative device our explosion of technical devices—ipods, notebooks, etc. We often call these "inspirations," rightly so, because to inspire is to breathe in, and the word for breath is the same word as "spirit" in the

Scriptures. Thus, something inspired comes from the spiritual realm.

Besides creating from inspiration, the spirit also receives information from a spiritual dimension through his intuition. Through this facility, his spirit functions within the natural world as well, sensing the spirits of other individuals. Corinthians 2:11 says, "For what man knoweth the things of a man save the spirit of man which is in him?" But the spirit can also function by receiving input from the evil spiritual world, especially when taught the ways and means by demonic doctrines, hence the laws forbidding traffic with demons.

The natural man—as he is born—cannot receive spiritual revelation from God through his spirit, because of original sin brought on by the fall of Adam and Eve. Paul confirms this in I Corinthians. 4:14 where he says, "But the natural man receiveth not the things of the Spirit of God . . . because they are spiritually discerned." God requires a cleansed spirit, that is, one free from the guilt of sin [a clear conscience], for communication. The natural man's conscience is so defiled that his spirit is said to be "dead in trespasses and sins" (Ephesians. 2:1 AV).

This condition proves no difficulty to the demonic spirits, however, for they are attracted to sin, and provide great input to the souls of men via the spirit. That is what James meant when he said men are drawn away of their "own lust and enticed." Demons entice. The newspapers are full of incidents in which crimes are committed as a result of "urges" overcoming the lawbreakers. David Wilkerson, former head of the Times Square Church in New York City, mentioned in one of his cover letters about the powerful "urges to kill" confessed to him by those he sought to counsel. He sees more demon activity in the inner city now than all his many years of ministry. In a vacuum of God's positive spiritual input, demons have reached many spirits via the intuition with negative spiritual influence.

We have looked at how the creative imagination and intuition work with the soul. Later we will look at the worship and conscience channel when we deal with the spirit in more detail. However, because of the importance of the intuition to a man's destiny, we digress here to take up:

The Consequences of Choice

The intuitive sense comes alive to God when a person hears the good news that Jesus, God's spotless Son, died to remove the sin penalty from all mankind. First, he hears, and then understands with his mind that "all have sinned and come short of the glory of God" (Romans 3:23 AV), which includes himself. Next he becomes convicted in his conscience for past wrongdoing, and decides to change [repent].

He actively chooses first, to believe what the Bible says about his own sin; and second, to accept God's offer of salvation by letting God's perfect sacrifice for all sin become his own offering before a righteous and holy God. He seals his choice by confessing/*declaring* Jesus as his Savior with his mouth.

His act of faith in believing what God says in the Bible about sin, himself, and damnation, cancels the record of his sin in heaven. At the same time, his spirit feels the clearing of his conscience as the Holy Spirit joins Himself to his spirit, birthing in him a new attitude toward life. With his conscience cleansed, his spiritual channel is now open to God. He begins to perceive a communication with the Holy

Spirit, who will continue to dwell in him. Through his cleared intuition, he receives instruction, direction, and great joy, accompanied by feelings of love and acceptance.

Or contrarily, if a person chooses not to believe what the Scriptures say about him or his sin debt he may override the feelings of guilt by justifying his lifestyle and by hardening his heart against the information about God. Each one chooses what he will believe, *not by the facts*, but by his own desires.

If he rejects God's offer to remove his sins through Christ's substitutionary death, then his spirit remains dead toward God. The channel remains closed except to demons. Therefore, it is a man's soul, or more specifically his heart, through its influence over his will, that ultimately determines the eternal destiny of each man.

A man's own stubborn self-will explains why otherwise intelligent persons continue to reject God's offer of salvation and cleansing. Driven by pride and a thorough determination to do their own thing, they decide against God's offer and damn their own souls. Or they may make an unconscious choice by ignoring God altogether, through a lack of interest. They never realize their accountability to Him. Jesus said no man could come to Him unless the Father draw him (by attraction? like a magnet? John 6:44). Thus, the eternal destiny of each person lies in his own choice, or lack of it, for although the soul has a beginning, it has no end. It dwells in the spirit, which is also eternal and will inhabit a body designed for the habitation in its eternal dwelling place (Matthew 10:28). In heaven, one's new body given at resurrection 1 Corinthians 15:51-54; 2 Corinthians 5:1) remains immortal to match his eternal life given at his salvation (Ephesians 1:13, 14; John 10:27, 28).

The apostle Paul calls the receiving of a new body "an adoption" in Romans 8:23--"even we ourselves groan within ourselves, waiting for the adoption, to wit, the redemption of our body." God redeems the spirit the moment one accepts His grace. He redeems the soul over a lifetime as each tries to change his selfish nature into God's own character through instruction of the kingdom laws and help from the Holy Spirit. God does not redeem the body until the resurrection.

Speaking of the body, the apostle John tells us in 1 John 3:2, "Now beloved, we are the sons of God, and it doth not yet appear what we shall be: but we know that, when he shall appear, we shall be like him; for we shall see him as he is." Here, John is not talking about Jesus' virtue, but His resurrected body. That body operated in both the natural and spiritual dimensions.

Except for the transfiguration, the disciples only saw Jesus in the natural realm. After His resurrection, they saw him in a body that could materialize with ease from the spiritual realm to the physical realm. Believers will have the same new body as he. They will move in both dimensions, because they will live in both dimensions with Christ. About their existence in the spiritual realm Paul says, "we shall judge angels" (1 Corinthians. 6:3). About the natural realm, Revelation 5:10 says that the redeemed will be kings and priests over the earth. Both supply endless blessing.

In contrast, the unredeemed person having received a body able to register constant pain (Luke 16:19-25), will live on and on in agony in Hell in utter despair of his soul.

Jesus told His disciples, "And fear not them which kill the body, but are not able to kill the soul: but rather fear him [God] which is able to destroy both soul and body in hell"[1] (Matthew 10:28AV). Like Paul, "knowing the terror of the Lord, we persuade men . . ." (2 Corinthians. 5:11), because each man's personal destiny lies in his own soul's choice. The stakes are high, too high to risk not understanding them.

Having understood that the resurrected body is also eternal (saved, or condemned to God's garbage dump for worthless lives), let us return to how the body soul and spirit work together.

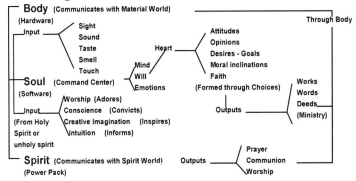

Diagram of the Soul

From the diagram we can see that the body and the spirit both gather input for the soul. Even so, it's the body that accomplishes all activity. Another analogy might be the body is like a car, with the soul as its driver and the spirit as its fuel. All are necessary, but it's the car that gets the driver where he's going.

The Modes of the Soul

---

[1] Mary Kay Baxter' gives testimony that she was shown souls hell, each occupying his own pit of fire where his body covered with worms was destroyed over and over again as fire came upon him burning the flesh off his eternal body. Its flesh was then restored only to have the whole process begin again.

The Bible uses conflicting expressions to refer to the soul. It speaks of "the natural man" versus "the spiritual man," "the old man" versus "the new man," and "the flesh" versus "the Spirit" [of God] in man. These describe different modes that the soul can assume. The "natural man" describes the state of all men. All are born in sin, which motivates independence and rebellion against God. This condition results from original sin committed by Adam and passes down to all descendants. We see an example of this in any young child asserting his independence from authority. Independence comes naturally, but obedience must be learned.

Another example is lying. Do we set down Sally and say, "Today I'm going to teach you how to lie." No, we don't. Do children lie? You had better believe they do! It just comes naturally.

Because of this, "natural man" is born cut off from God in his spirit. Paul told the Corinthians: "But the natural man does not receive the things of the Spirit of God, for they are foolishness to him; nor can he know them, because they are spiritually discerned. But he who is spiritual judges all things, yet he himself is rightly judged by no one." On the other hand the "spiritual man" is the "born again" man whose spirit was vitalized by the Holy Spirit at salvation, and is now alive toward God and considered a son in the family of God (2 Corinthians. 2:14, 15 NKJV).

The "spiritual man," "the new man" and "the Spirit," who leads the new man, are the same mode. "The old man" and "the flesh" are expressions of "the natural man," which *are still dormant* in one who receives a spiritual rebirth. In other words, the redeemed person now has two natures—an old one and a new one. The story is told of a native who received Jesus and went home rejoicing. Later he became perplexed and returned to the missionary for help. He said, "Now I have two dogs inside of me, who are always fighting. A white dog that wants me to do good, and a black dog that wants me to go back to doing evil." This calls to mind the cartooned picture of the devil sitting on one shoulder and an angel on the other whispering to the man as to what to do. Both draw attention to the conflicting natures.

The believer, commonly called a Christian, can operate in either mode. He can do his own will, which is also in line with the devil, or the will of the Father as shown by the Holy Spirit. This is why non-Christians often make the claim that all Christians are hypocrites. Too often they observe Christians in the mode of the flesh, living the same as the rest of the world. The Scriptures proclaim the will of the Father for righteous living in the laws of the kingdom. The surrounding world dictates to "the flesh" by enticements and flattery. The Apostle John says that the love of the world (the ways of general society), are in rebellion against God. All of this is contrary to the love of the Father.

> **"Do not love the world or the things in the world. If anyone loves the world, the love of the Father is not in him. For all that is in the world—the lust of the flesh, the lust of the eyes, and the pride of life—is not of the Father but is of the world."**
>
> **1 John 2:15, 16 NKJV**

World's Values

Lust of the Flesh----I feel (Good)--------------------Spirit/Body
Lust of the Eyes-----I want (Money, Things, People)----Will
Pride of Life----------I am (Somebody Great)------Soul/Mind

The "lust of the flesh" appeals to the emotions and the appetites of the flesh, clamoring for satisfaction of its delights. Some examples might be excesses in food and drink, or drugs to give the body or the spirit highs, or excessive or indulging in perverted sex. Thus the world's values and "the flesh" represent the same mode as the diagram shows. Feeling good physically satisfies "the flesh."

Perhaps this is the reason eating is such a comfort to dissatisfied souls. These are things for which the flesh lusts.

The "lust of the eyes" fulfills the selfish nature—the desire for things or people or purposes to our liking. Envy often fuels this lust. The "pride of life" is the desire to be elevated and recognized. It manifests as a lust for the power of influence over others.

On the other hand, the soul in the mode of the spiritual man has his heart set upon another direction, to please God rather than himself, which leads to pleasing self in a good way. Paul explains that the goal of all teaching is to produce ". . . love out of a pure heart and a good conscience and faith unfeigned" (1 Timothy 1:5 NKJV).

Look at the difference between the world and the freedom of God's ways.

```
Pure heart------------Mind----------------Free of sinful thoughts
Faith unfeigned-----Will----------------Trusts in God's choices
Clear conscience----Emotions------------------Free to enjoy life
```

In his famous Basic Youth Conflicts Seminars, Bill Gothard teaches that all problems in life can be traced to one of three root causes: immorality, temporal values, or bitterness. By keeping our souls in the mode of "the spiritual man," we can avoid these problems.

The pure heart won't respond to immoral stimuli. The fully assured, faith-filled heart looks at things from an eternal perspective and isn't impressed with the world's value system. The repentant or forgiving heart keeps such a clear conscience that bitterness has little chance of developing.

Canceling Root Causes

```
Immorality----------------------Canceled by---------------------------Pure Heart
Bitterness------------------------Canceled by Forgiveness---Cleared Conscience
Temporal------------------------ -Canceled by God's Choices-----------True Faith
```

Think of the peace this philosophy can bring to a life! Contrasting the righteous mode with the mode of "the flesh," we find just the opposite. Of the three root causes, the "lust of the flesh" answers the call to all sorts of immoral stimuli. The "lust of the eyes" asks for, wants, and desires temporal pleasures to be met—now! The "pride of life" is easily offended and prone toward bitterness if people do not give him his due. So, to be spiritually successful in this world and avoid problems, the Christian's soul must stay in the mode of "the spiritual man" and avoid the mode of "the flesh."

Paul talked about these modes often. For instance, in the letter to the Ephesians he says:

> **This I say, therefore, and testify in the Lord, that you should no longer walk as the rest of the Gentiles walk, in the futility of their mind, having their understanding darkened, being alienated from the life of God, because of the ignorance that is in them, because of the blindness of their heart; who, being past feeling, have given themselves over to lewdness, to work all uncleanness with greediness.**

> But you have not so learned Christ, if indeed you have heard Him and have been taught by Him, as the truth is in Jesus: that you put off, concerning your former conduct, *the old man* which grows corrupt according to the deceitful lusts, and be renewed in the spirit of your mind, and that you put on the new man which was created according to God, in true righteousness and holiness.
>
> Therefore, putting away lying, "Let each one *of you* speak truth with his neighbor," for we are members of one another. "Be angry, and do not sin": do not let the sun go down on your wrath, nor give place to the devil. Let him who stole steal no longer, but rather let him labor, working with *his* hands what is good, that he may have something to give him who has need. Let no corrupt word proceed out of your mouth, but what is good for necessary edification, that it may impart grace to the hearers. And do not grieve the Holy Spirit of God, by whom you were sealed for the day of redemption. Let all bitterness, wrath, anger, clamor, and evil speaking be put away from you, with all malice. And be kind to one another, tenderhearted, forgiving one another, even as God in Christ forgave you.
>
> **Ephesians 4:24-31 NKJV**

The output of the two modes can be contrasted. The new man is renewed, his spirit being recreated through the input of the Holy Spirit. But letting "the old man" control the soul (and thus the mouth) grieves the Holy Spirit (Ephesians 4:29-31).

Now look at another letter:

> But now you must also rid yourselves of all such things as these: anger, rage, malice, slander, and filthy language from your lips. Do not lie to each other, since

> **you have taken off *your old self* with its practices and have *put on the new self*, which is being renewed in knowledge in the image of its Creator**
>
> **Colossians 3:8-10 NKJV**

This passage points out the same thing. The "old man" is prone to negative emotions and evil deeds, whereas the "new man" develops from the input of knowledge given through the Holy Spirit.

So we learn that not only is the Soul the controlling part of man, but also that it operates in two different modes. One mode loves and desires to please the Father. The other loves and desires to please self. Whichever way our souls go, our bodies and spirits will follow.

Knowing this, we understand why God wishes to capture our heart or soul. From the moment we are conceived, until the moment we die, our souls continue to develop. We either become righteous souls, unrighteous souls—or somewhere in between—according to our deeds. Paul said even we Christians will be judged for our deeds for they are the fruits growing out from our hearts.

Conclusion

The finished state of our souls is subject to judgment. Salvation, or lack of it, determines the place of judgment. The unsaved are judged at the great white throne (Revelation 20:11-15) where punishment is meted out to pay for their sinful deeds according to their level of evil. The saved are judged at the judgment seat of Christ (2 Corinthians 5:10) where rewards are given out for faithful service, their sins having already been canceled by the sacrifice of Jesus Christ.

Living in the mode of the flesh wastes spiritual life and forfeits eternal rewards. Therefore, it seems prudent for Christians to try to stay in the mode of the "new man." Since the consequence of how we live is eternal, we would all do well "to take heed unto our souls." The laws of the kingdom will help us to do that.

The Spirit Gives Life—Plus

In the diagram of the tri-part man, I illustrated the spirit as the power-producer of the man. I did this because I believe that the Bible teaches that first, the spirit of man is the power source for life. And second, I believe all energy to operate that life also comes from the spirit through its regulation.

Life always proceeds from life. As was mentioned in the last chapter, God breathed (put a spirit) into the formed dust, i.e. carbon, calcium, and sodium, etc., and man became a living soul. In this case, it was life from God that gave life to Adam.

When the body can no longer support life, the spirit leaves. Jarius called for Jesus to come and pray for his daughter, but she was already dead when he arrived. In Luke 8:55 when Jesus said, "Maid arise," the Scripture says, "And her spirit came again and she arose straightway." James states it flatly when he says, "For as the body without the spirit is dead . . ." (James 2:26). This was even true of the Lord Jesus, who had power over His own life. He laid it down of his own accord when He dismissed His own spirit.

> **And when Jesus had cried out with a loud voice, He said, "Father, 'into Your hands I commit My spirit.'" Having said this, He breathed His last.**
>
> Luke 23:46 NKJV

Later when the soldiers checked, they found Him already dead. His spirit had left His body earlier. So we can see from these three Scriptures that "life," according to the Bible, dwells in our spirits. When our physical bodies can no longer support life, our spirits leave, and our bodies die.

The Spirit Charges Our Emotions and Causes Our Moods

Besides giving a person life, the spirit also regulates all energy to operate that life. Of course, potential energy comes from eating, which produces the raw material for energy. Yet the emotions, affecting the spirit, cause its energy to fluctuate. We understand this from Proverbs 18:14, "The spirit of a man will sustain his infirmity; but a wounded spirit who can bear?"

Though a man is sick, the life in his spirit will sustain him, providing the body has the resources. But if his spirit is afflicted by negative emotions, he not only lowers his own energy but he also has an effect on others. Proverbs 17:22 is another example: "A merry heart doeth good like a medicine: but a *broken spirit* drieth the bones." The body responds to the spirit's energy level. Emotions also rise and fall according to the energy of the spirit and vice versa.

Thus when emotions break one's spirit, they affect his body (dry the bones), causing a drain on his system. One can affect others the same way. On the other hand, a cheerful spirit also infects others, lifting their spirits. Our own use of words says the same thing. Here are a few examples: Friday night before the big game on Saturday, students gather around a large bonfire. They come to cheer on their team. Cheerleaders shout, "We've got spirit! A horse quivers with excitement, nervously sidestepping and having to be tightly reigned by his rider. We call this a "spirited horse." A child excitedly bursts into a room exclaiming some good news. We say he is full of "high spirits."

These examples describe a high level of energy. Thus, the spirit charges our emotions and thereby determines our moods. While the soul may control what we do, the spirit controls *how we do it*. If we do it with a lot of energy, we're in "high spirits." If we drag and mope we're in "low spirits." The soul has its modes but the spirit has its moods. Looking at the diagram we see the indicator needle points to the heart's choice with corresponding results:

The Modes of the Soul as it Relates to the Spirit

World	God
Old man under	New Man
Spirit of disobedience	Walking in the Spirit

| Joy -Peace – Love | Pride, Self– |
| Resurrection–Power | Esteem, Lust |

The energy of the spirit works in either mode. The needle with arrows indicates the mode of the soul. In the diagram it points to the "new man," therefore the Holy Spirit fuels the spirit that in turn fuels the body. If he walks after the Holy Spirit in the new man, his esteem comes from knowing who he is in God, and it doesn't matter what the world thinks of him. His energy comes from being accepted in the "Beloved," and the power of Jesus' resurrected life sustains him daily. The joy of the Lord is his strength.

The only other thing that can dampen the spirit is physical pain or sickness in the body, which lowers energy physically, but faith can overcome it, if he truly walks in the Spirit.

But if one walks after the world in the mode of the flesh, the spirit fuels his body according to his self-esteem or pleasant prospects. The energy level can be high or low. If prospects are good, much energy flows. If they are bad, just the opposite happens. The flesh is subject to the values of the world and therefore fluctuates accordingly. The flesh can draw much power from sin. Lust and pride are packed with destructive power that will eventually destroy the entire man, body, soul and spirit.

**The Spirit Displays Our Character
To Others**

The heart displays its attitudes in the spirit through body language. The reason: because the spirit moves the body. Body language is just that—body language. "What you do speaks so loud I cannot hear what you are saying," says the same thing. Proverbs mentions "a proud look" as one of the things God hates. What is that but body language? Some time ago the TV ran a commercial advertising a sweet treat made from a leading cereal. The commercial used what is called reverse psychology to emphasize how easily the recipe could be made. The woman in the commercial said, "Go ahead, eat the last piece. I can make some more. I don't mind. Really."

But her voice inflection and her body language revealed just the opposite. She lacked enthusiasm and it was obvious that she minded very much. Her actions spoke louder than her words.

The Scriptures abound with examples of attitude or character depicted in the spirit. In the list below, try to imagine the action that tips off the attitude in each spirit. Psalm 78:8 talks about a spirit that is not steadfast. Could this be a body displaying restlessness? Psalm 32:2 speaks of a spirit without guile—an open and truthful spirit? Proverbs 16:18 mentions a haughty spirit. Here, we would naturally think of an up-turned nose. And so the list goes on. Proverbs 16:19, a humble spirit; Ecclesiastes 7:8, a patient spirit; I Peter 3:4, a meek and quiet spirit; Galatians 6:1, a spirit of meekness. In Luke 9:55, Jesus warned James and John that they did not know what spirit they were of, because they wanted to call fire down on a village that rejected Jesus. They displayed a vengeful spirit.

Proverbs 16:2 tells a sobering fact. It says:

"All the ways of a man are clean in his own eyes, but the Lord weighs the spirits." The spirit acts out the attitudes in our heart, and collectively these acts display our character. God judges character. Because of this, the spirit affects all three parts of our souls. It strengthens our will, charging it with purpose or just the opposite. (Its power can even destroy the will to live.) The spirit renovates the mind with truth and revelation knowledge from the Holy Spirit; or the spirit clutters it with deception and confusion from unholy spirits. The spirit causes our emotions to rejoice and soar; or it causes them to groan, sigh or grieve.

Thus, the spirit regulates the very life force of a person. It also produces all the operating energy, and by charging our emotions, causes our moods, and displays our character. This is why we say the spirit of man is the power pack of the whole being.

The Spirit Acts as an Input/Output Channel Like the Body

First, we will look at input channels. Just as the body communicates with the material world of nature, the spirit communicates with the spiritual world of energy. Like the body, the spirit has input and output that come and go from the command center, the soul. The input channels, as we showed in the diagram of the tri-part being, are Worship, Conscience, Creative Imagination, and Intuition. The output channels are Communion (a part of Worship) and Prayer (which can also be a part of worship).

Worship

The Worship channel is the built-in need of a human being to worship something. Often described as a hole in one's being that only God can fill, this spiritual aptitude constitutes a search for the meaning of life—a reason for being.

Besides worshipping the true God, men satisfy this need in various other ways. They make gods from stone and wood, which resemble a demon that has materialized briefly, promising power, prosperity or protection in exchange for worship. Ancient men worshipped the planets. The days of the week are named for them. Or, they may worship great men or political leaders, elevating them as gods. The many statues of Lenin replaced gods in Russia's Communistic Atheism. Secular Humanism delivers the ultimate insult to God because it makes mankind with his achievements the object of worship. But worship something they must, because worship justifies human existence. Therefore, every man worships something, whether admitted or not, if he only worships himself.

True worship, however, depends on one's knowledge of the only true God who made heaven and earth, and fulfills the desire to appreciate Him. Jesus, speaking to the Samaritan woman (John 4:24), said that His Father seeks those who worship Him to worship in spirit and in truth. This entails our spirits seeking to adore the God revealed in the Holy Scriptures (the truth) by the power of His Holy Spirit .

Conscience

Conscience, the second inputting channel, has just one function. It registers guilt for perceived wrongdoing and sends painful misgivings through the emotions. Keeping the conscience clear is a major part of the Christian walk. We refer again to Paul's declaration to Timothy (1 Timothy 1:5) that the goal of all teaching is to teach men how to have a pure heart, a clear conscience and a true faith. Thus, teaching men to have a clear conscience was equally as important as teaching them to have a pure heart, or a true faith. Sin destroys the intimate relationship with the Father. John says, "Beloved, if our heart condemn us not, then we have confidence toward God" (1 John 3:21).

Men do strange things to cover a guilty conscience. They blame others. They do other deeds to try to compensate, or they do penance, sometimes inflicting themselves with physical pain. Of course, none of these actions clear the conscience, because only admission of guilt and subsequent forgiveness will clear a guilty conscience (1 John 1:8, 9) and only to those who have been absolved of their sins by Christ's death.

A guilty conscience affects the body as well as the soul. Lie detector tests depend on this. When a man lies, the body reacts because of a guilty conscience. His blood pressure rises, and his electrical impulses reflect a reaction on the machine. The Kikuyu tribe in Kenya determined who was telling the truth by laying a hot knife to the tongue of the accused. The innocent person did not fear detection, since he was not guilty. However, the conscience of the guilty dried out his tongue, and it burned. Thus the guilty were quickly discerned.

Old Testament law gives a similar case. If a man suspected his wife of infidelity, he could take her to the priest who performed the offering of jealousy. The priest took clean water and put dust from the ground in it. He then pronounced a curse and gave it to the woman to drink. If she was free from the charge, she was free from the curse. But if guilty, it would cause her thigh to rot and her belly to swell (Leviticus 5:21). Apparently, her guilty conscience destroyed her body's immune system. Because much power lies in the spirit, Scripture exhorts us to keep our consciences clear, so that we may escape the negative use of this power.

There are three types of consciences—the natural conscience, the trained conscience, and the seared conscience.

1. The natural conscience, the one we are born with, is like a blank page waiting for someone to write the rules. It can learn by default by accepting the convictions of his environment, his family, his neighborhood, or his ethnic group. Some rules may be good, others not (Romans 2:15). This conscience responds to conviction of wrong behavior to the learned code. A young child's tender conscience can be quickly prejudiced by the teaching of negative environments such as ethnic hatreds where it becomes all right to slander or even murder those hated.

2. The trained conscience learns by strong teachings—usually religious—and responds when some rule has been broken. Whether the rules are from teachings or decisions made from the individual's own convictions, they still bring guilt. Psychologists sometimes try to get rid of guilt by getting rid of rules. But this does not work, because the only way a trained conscience can be changed is by retraining; i.e., replacing the rules with other rules. Good training depends on an understanding of what God considers right and wrong behavior. This comes from the standard of the Word of God, the Bible, which is full of behavioral laws. Further, the Word declares God will judge and punish all those who break his laws, charging the conscience with a healthy fear of God (Ecclesiastes. 12:13, 14; Revelation 20:12,). Therefore, it is paramount that believers know the word of God to the extent that they know how to behave.

Poor training of the conscience depends upon legalistic convictions of men. These, come from perversions of the written word, whether it's the Bible, the Koran or any other religious text and are not the intent of that writing. Therefore, we have variants of sects and their behavioral limitations or lack thereof (Islamic terrorists, Judaic Right terrorists, Christian militaristic terrorists, etc.). Such a conscience also tends to condemn others whose behavior breaks the rules to which they have subscribed.

Even sincere Christians, who are trying to obey the letter of the law, without understanding its intent, bring bondage upon themselves and others. On the other hand, understanding the intent by the Spirit brings liberty and a right conscience.

3. A seared or burned-out conscience describes one that has sinned repeatedly, knowing full well God's standard. Such a conscience forms spiritual "scar tissue" from the constant burning of guilt, which makes it rigid or seared, like burn-scarred skin. Without flexibility a conscience cannot function. When sin no longer registers, any behavior becomes acceptable to that conscience, for there is no inner voice to stop him.

This, condition poses a dangerous situation, because a soul without the warning of conscience is like a body whose nervous system does not feel pain. Such a body can receive fatal injury and never know it.

Demons, as well as the apostate leaders of the church, are said to have seared consciences (1 Timothy 4:1, 2). These forgo redemption, since they are without conviction of sin, and therefore will not repent.

So the conscience serves as a vital part of the spirit. But Holy Spirit must train it with God's standard if it is to be completely effective.

Creative Imagination

The third input channel is the creative imagination. Perhaps this facility of the spirit demonstrates our being made in the image of God more than the others. While the ability to worship gives us a capacity to enjoy God and enter into the things that delight Him, and the conscience gives us discernment of wrong behavior, the creative imagination gives us the ability to imitate Him. Just as a child delights in mimicking his father, so we also take pleasure in creating.

Genesis 1:1 says, "In the beginning God created the heavens and the earth . . ." and later states that creation was the work of God (Genesis. 2:2). After each creation God pronounced that it was good. In other words, He took pleasure and satisfaction from His efforts. He also took His identity from His work. He is known as the God who created the heavens and the earth (Psalms 146:5, 6; 2 Chronicles. 2:12). Men appreciate Him, because what He has done reveals the power and majesty of His person.

The same is true of us. The creative imagination is our ability and, indeed, our need to work. We, like God, also receive pleasure and satisfaction in our accomplishments. Yes, and also our identity. For example, when we think of Thomas Edison, we think of the electric light bulb. When we think of Alexander Graham Bell, we think of the telephone. Works make men stand out. Sin perverts the need to work. Laziness denies the man of the benefits of work. Proverbs 10:4 says, "He becometh poor that dealeth with a slack hand, but the hand of the diligent maketh rich." And again Proverbs 13:4 says, "The soul of the sluggard desireth, and hath nothing: but the soul of the diligent shall be made fat." Satisfaction of accomplishment as well as fiscal benefits is denied the lazy man.

Dishonesty perverts the God-given instinct to work. All ill-gotten gain denies the rights of others. Stealing takes from the diligent and gives to the lazy, who use their creative powers illegitimately. Proverbs 4:16 tells us, "For they sleep not, except they have done mischief; and their sleep is taken away, unless they cause someone to fall." All planning, inventing, designing, or problem solving originates in the spirit, which inspires the mind and activates the body. This capacity greatly contributes to our happiness. Even Adam, who was put in a perfect environment, was given work to do in Eden. Enjoyment and satisfaction of life, as well as a healthy self-esteem, come from our accomplishments.

Paul exhorts the Galatians to have compassion on those with spiritual burdens who need consoling, but let each to bear their own burden when it comes to labor (Galatians 6:2-5). He specifically says concerning work, "For if a man think himself to be something, when he is nothing, he deceiveth himself. But let every man prove his own work, and then shall he have rejoicing in himself alone, and not in another." His satisfaction comes from accomplishment rather than compliments from others.

Intuition

The fourth input channel of the spirit is intuition. This is the ability to know; i.e., impart to the mind knowledge, without the use of the body's senses. This information comes across spiritual channels similar to the way radio waves transverse the atmosphere. Like little receivers tuned toward the spiritual realm, our spirits pick up broadcasts unconsciously according to their inclination. If I point the tuner of my radio toward 750 on the dial, I get WSB Atlanta, but if I tune it to 860, I get CNN. If we tune our spirits toward God, we receive through the Holy Spirit. If we tune our spirits to the world, we pick up the "prince of the power of the air, the spirit that now worketh in the children of disobedience" (Ephesians. 2:2).

The broadcasts come in the form of thoughts or sometimes words. It can be just the sensing of another person's spirit, like Jesus, when he said to the palsied man, "Your sins are forgiven," or perceived in His spirit the thoughts of the Pharisees condemning Him of blasphemy. He immediately asked them, "Is it easier to say pick up thy bed and walk or thy sins be forgiven thee?" (Mark 2:8). Or like Peter, when he declared that Jesus was "the Christ, the Son of the living God," and Jesus declared "flesh and blood hath not revealed it unto thee, but my Father who is in heaven" (Matthew 16:17).

Evil thoughts, constantly broadcast by Satan and his demons, also come via spiritual channels. For this reason Paul said we should make every thought captive to the Lord (1 Corinthians 10:5).

We should also try the spirits of teachers, because spiritual knowledge given to them via their intuition is then passed along to us. Anointed teachers give forth teaching from the Holy Spirit, while false teachers give forth teaching from unholy spirits, themselves being deceived. Of course, some teaching comes from the human mind (soul), which may contain error due to lack of knowledge. *All teaching* is, at best, a mixture

We try the spirits by intuition. The Holy Spirit within us recognizes what is from him and confirms it to our spirits (providing we know the fundamentals of our faith). If the teaching is off base, an alarm goes off, and we sense a troubling in our spirit, breaking its peace. Therefore, even the teaching received from others is revealed as truth or rejected as false by our intuition.

Intuition discerns the doctrines of demons. The Scriptures tell us that dangerous false teaching denies the coming of Christ in the flesh (1 John 4:3). Such teaching always comes couched in subtlety, so, it too, must be discerned in the spirit via intuition.

Individual study guided by the Holy Spirit brings growth and spiritual maturity to our understanding. Called "revelation knowledge," this too comes by the input channel of intuition, especially in those gifted to teach. Teachers, by individual study and the sharing of their discovered truth in ministry, edify the whole body of Christ.

The Holy Spirit sometimes operates through one's intuition to bring supernatural power to the Church in the form of spiritual gifts. Called "power gifts," there are nine in all. They include three knowing gifts: a word of knowledge, a word of wisdom, and the discerning of spirits; three doing gifts: gifts of healings, miracles and faith; and three speaking gifts: speaking in tongues, interpretation of tongues and prophecy.

The Holy Spirit uses these gifts on special occasions (according to his own working) to bring especially called individuals or whole fellowships to greater understanding, greater faith, or greater direction.

For example, Paul and Barnabus went out as missionaries from Antioch as a result of a prophetic word given by someone in their group while they were praying. The Scripture simply states that the Holy Ghost said, "Separate me Barnabus and Saul for the work whereunto I have called them" (Acts 13:2). One in their midst spoke the word to the whole group. He heard the words in his spirit and voiced them by prophesying. Everyone present responded in obedience, because each recognized the words as a message from the Holy Spirit.

An example of a word of knowledge might be Peter's discernment of Ananias and Sapphira's lie about the sale of their property (Acts 5:1-11). Peter had no way of knowing that they had conspired together except that the Holy Spirit revealed it to him in "a word of knowledge." Bob Mumford, during a stint when he was teaching in a Seminary was sitting in the bathtub when the Holy Spirit revealed to him some sin his students were engaged in. He immediately got out of the tub and dressed. He went to their dormitory and confronted the guilty parties. The look on the faces confirmed the truth. That incidence put the fear of God in the whole body of students, knowing that God would tell on them.

An Old Testament example of the same thing would be in the story of Elisha healing Naaman (2 Kings 5). Although Elisha declined payment, his servant Gahazi followed after and lied to Naaman to get gain for himself. When he returned, Elisha asked Gahazi where he had been.

Gahazi lied again when he said, "Your servant went no whither." But God had shown it unto Elisha, so he retorted, "Went not my heart with thee, when the man turned again from his chariot to meet thee?" God supernaturally revealed the dealings Gahazi had with Naaman.

The power gift for healings can come from the Holy Spirit and through the intuition as well. Sometimes the one ministering healing hears a word of knowledge telling him exactly what infirmities God is healing in an assembly of believers. Minnie Coleman was such a one. My twenty plus year old son was healed from a weakness to succumb to throat infections when she spoke that ailment.

Other times healing passes from the ministering one, to the sick one body to body, by the "laying on" of hands.

Signs and wonders often accompany the gospel through the ministry of the workers in revivals or missionary efforts. These, display visible evidences of the power of God to save. Thousands have been saved in Africa in the last decades because of the miraculous power of the Holy Spirit manifesting in spiritual gifts. An African pastor told the visiting worker, Mahesh Shavda, "You know of course, the crowds would not come if there were no miracles. But miracles abounded. Sick and dying were healed, demons were cast out, and the dead arose. All this was accomplished through spiritual gifts that operated by words. Instruction, given from the Holy Spirit to the minister through his intuition, inspired his faith. Obedience to those words caused God's power to be manifested in miracles, healing, or deliverance. Mark 16:17-18 tells us that these signs should follow the preaching of the gospel.

However, the Spirit of God is not the only spirit that can communicate through the intuition. Although limited when compared with God's power, counterfeit power gifts come from unholy spirits the same way. The witch doctor has gifts of healing and words of knowledge. Psychic mediums "channel" to the spiritual realm for information on the behalf of others. They seek knowledge by the power of demons—though they may not know it.

Since the demons see all that goes on in the material world present or past, the demons are full of information. Psychics believe that the information comes from some greater consciousness. They are deceived. The power of this seductive teaching prevents those under its influence from seeing the truth. For this reason, traffic with demons (psychic power) is strictly forbidden in the Scriptures.

Christians who stumble into the occult without realizing the danger pick up demonic influences. These, lodge in their spirits and must be purged out if the intuition is to operate freely with God's Spirit. Paul admonishes the Christians in Corinth to cleanse themselves "from all filthiness of flesh and spirit, perfecting holiness in the fear of God" (2 Corinthians. 7:1). Flesh here refers to the mode of the soul; therefore, the exhortation says to cleanse our souls and our spirits. This statement shows that both the soul *and the spirit* can be defiled even after salvation.

The Output Channels—Communion and Prayer

The spirit has two output channels: Communion and Prayer. These channels issue from intuition, or worship, or both. Communion comes from the word "commune," which means to converse or share intimately. Communion with God joins spirits, sharing intimately in the spirit. Paul said that he that is joined to God is one spirit (1 Corinthians. 6:17). He compared spiritual communion to the intimacy of a joining in the flesh. Since God the Father is Spirit, being joined in spirit with Him is truly like a joining of flesh to flesh, only in this case it is spirit to Spirit. Perhaps this is the reason God calls joining with an unholy spirit by venturing into the occult, or dabbling with Spiritism, spiritual adultery.

The worship channel inputs the inspiration for worship and outputs the act of worship through communion. It's a communication. We tell God our appreciation of His person, His might, His righteousness, and His mercy; and we receive back His approval and acceptance of our worship.

Our whole being gets involved—body and soul as well as the spirit—even though the spirit directs by inspiration. We sing praises with our mouths, clap and raise our hands and sometimes bow down our whole bodies in an act of worship. Our minds and emotions are overcome with the awe of our God, and his majesty; and our bodies respond to our spirits with appropriate body language.

Prayer

Prayer also involves exchanges between God and man. But prayer is more need-oriented, while communion is more praise-oriented. Communion brings satisfaction to the desire to worship. Prayer, especially answered prayer, brings faith and knowledge of God's power, which in turn inspires more worship by thanksgiving.

Prayer offers God more opportunity to work, and for mankind, a chance to work in cooperation with Him. Since God sets limits upon Himself and gives men a measure of free will, He will seldom interfere in our lives unless we ask Him to (James 4:2; John 16:24; Ezekiel. 22:30). Prayer, especially intercessory prayer (Scripture calls this standing in the gap), opens a will for God to act upon. Without prayer the spiritual enemies of God run largely unchecked, because prayer hinders their activity. God is sovereign in the control of history, but God's permissive will allows a lot of latitude in the individual lives of people. God is looking for intercessors, because He has chosen to run His kingdom by prayer.

Prayer then is asking God for something and outputting the request through our spirit to God's Spirit. Communion is offering our love through our spirit to the Holy Spirit. Both bring a joy to the heart of God.

In summary, the spirit is like the body in that it possesses sensors to discern its environment, the spiritual realm. With these sensors it inputs and outputs to and from the soul. The worship channel causes a man to worship his God/god and outputs communion, praise, and thanksgiving prayer. The conscience channel judges the man's heart and actions. The creative channel inspires work and accomplishment. The intuition channel inputs information and gifts supernaturally, and outputs prayer for ministry and intercession.

The Spirit Possesses Its Own Body

Yes, that's right. The spirit possesses its own body. It is interesting how many things we read and accept in Scripture without really understanding their implications. The spiritual body is an example. Paul tells us plainly that *there is* a natural body and *there is* a spiritual body (1 Corinthians. 15:44), but we assume that he means in the future because he talks about the resurrection in that chapter. A closer look, however, at the experiences of Ezekiel in the Old Testament and John in the New Testament, bear out the fact that we have a spiritual body and a natural body.

Beginning in chapter eight, and running through chapter eleven, Ezekiel relates a visionary experience. It begins in his own house before the elders whom, we assume, have come to hear him. But suddenly the Spirit of

God comes upon him, and the supernatural or spiritual supersedes the natural.

As we examine this experience, please note the references to some part of the body. First he sees a glorious form, which puts forth his hand and lifts Ezekiel by a lock of his hair. By the Spirit, the form lifts him (his whole body?) into space. Then it carries him to Jerusalem just inside the temple, where the Spirit tells Ezekiel to use his eyes to look at an idol. From there, the Spirit carries Ezekiel to the door of the court where he is asked to look at a hole in the wall. Then the Spirit tells him to dig (with his hands?) in the hole. After Ezekiel finds a secret door in the wall, the Spirit commands him to go in (walk in on his own power on his legs?) and behold the wicked abominations performed there.

Later in chapter nine, a voice cries in Ezekiel's ears with a loud voice. In chapter eleven, he is commanded to prophesy (with his mouth?). When observing the death of a prince after he had prophesied, Ezekiel fell down (his whole body?) upon his face. And finally, after an encouraging word concerning the future of Israel, the Spirit of God returns him to Chaldea, to those of the captivity he had been with when the Spirit took him away. The vision goes up from him and he returns to his natural body.

Meanwhile, during the time his was gone, the elders must have noticed the vacancy of his spirit. His natural body must have appeared as in a trance.

Did he only see this vision like one who experiences a realistic dream, or did he actually go to Jerusalem? Ezekiel 8:3 states, "And he put forth the form of an hand, and took me by a lock of mine head; and the spirit lifted me up between the earth and the heaven, and brought me in the visions of God to Jerusalem . . ." That was his exit from Chaldea. The interesting thing here is the hand. If Ezekiel's physical body was lifted up and carried to Jerusalem, then the hand would have been a physical hand. That is not likely. Most probably the hand was spiritual, seen only in the spirit realm. Ezekiel's mention of "in the visions of God" simply indicates that he knew the experience was spiritual." Therefore the body it picked up would have been Ezekiel's spirit body.

Then Ezekiel 11:24 states: "Afterwards, the spirit took me up, and brought me in a vision by the Spirit of God into Chaldea, to them of the captivity." This was his return to Chaldea. If God had wanted to show him what was happening in Jerusalem, he could have done this without any reference to Ezekiel's coming or going. Daniel received all kinds of visions without going anywhere. I believe God took Ezekiel to Jerusalem in his spirit body, so that he could be an actual eyewitness to the sins of Israel and report it to those he left in his house. Later, the Holy Spirit carried Ezekiel to the valley of dry bones, and still later, to a high mountain in the land of Israel, where he showed him the Millennial Temple. So we can conclude that God did not just show him pictures of future events but also took his spirit body to the location of these future events.

Now let's look at the example of the Apostle John. When John was in the spirit on the Lord's Day on Patmos, he saw a vision of the Lord standing among the lamp stands. He participated by seeing, falling down and writing what he heard. All this takes place on Patmos. Then, at the end of that vision, he sees a door open in heaven and a voice commands him to come up. It is here that John explains, "And immediately I was in the spirit . . . " In this state he sees, hears, weeps; takes a book from an angel, puts it in his mouth and tastes it, swallows it and feels bitterness in his belly. Then he stands on a mountain on the earth to observe the heavenly city descend. Being overcome with the glory of it all, he erroneously falls down to worship an angel. He does all these things while being in his spirit.

Paul was caught up to heaven also, and he plainly states that he could not tell whether he was in his body or out of it. Yet he testified that he saw and heard. He was not the least bit hindered in his capacities in the spiritual realm, any more than in the natural realm. His mind still received input, showing that while in the spirit his soul was also present. The same could be said of Ezekiel.

Having looked at Ezekiel and John's experiences in the spirit, let's go back to Paul's statement. "There is a natural body and there is a spiritual body. He knew this because he had experienced it. The Scripture does not say there will be, but *there is—now—*a spiritual body. The spiritual body is apparently made up of energy which forms at conception and grows to maturity. The testimonies of saints who have seen glimpses of eternity tell us that the spirits of infants who die grow up to maturity in heaven. But once mature they never age. The spirit body does not age on earth either. That is why we feel so young even with an aging natural body.

The natural spirit body becomes the pattern for the resurrection of the redeemed resurrected body that is like Jesus' resurrected body. Paul compares it to a natural grain seed (1 Corinthians 15:35-38). The plant grows until it produces seed. The seed does not look anything like the original plant as far as the natural eye can see, but the DNA of its life (the plant's vitality) is preserved to bring forth a new plant that looks exactly like the mother plant.

A man's spirit is invisible to the natural world, but when energized by the Holy Spirit, a man's spirit receives and *retains* eternal life. Passing through natural death does not change its original shape and features at maturity. (Distortions of an aging body have nothing to do with the spirit.) Thus, it becomes the pattern for the new body fitted to live in both worlds.

Paul says we will know even as we are known when we see Him face to face (1 Corinthians 13:12). How are we known? We will be known by our spirit bodies, partly because they resembled our physical bodies on earth and partly because the soul dwells in the spirit body. We identify one another today both by outward appearance and personality. The soul (containing the very heart of a man), dwells inside the spirit body just as the spirit body dwells inside the physical body. We know this truth because of the experiences of Ezekiel, Paul and John. They admitted to being in the spirit, but they also described thoughts and feelings, indicative of the soul.

A glove aptly describes this spiritual fit. Just as the hand fits inside the glove so the spirit body fits inside the natural body. When the glove moves, it is the hand inside that moves it. When the spirit is absent, the body lies limp like a discarded glove. But without the soul, there would not have been direction or motivation in Ezekiel or John. So the soul moves the spirit, and the spirit moves the physical body.

Many testimonies of saints tell of being in the spirit. Most of these are near death or clinical death experiences where the spirit leaves the body temporarily. Some have been carried into the heavenly realms, like John and Paul. Others have wandered on earth for short periods. In every case both the spiritual and the physical worlds were visible to them. They were aware of hands and feet and could see and hear. They possessed bodies that not only could walk about as their physical bodies, but also could travel through the air with accelerated speed to any place they wished to be. They could not communicate with the material world, however, for their hands would pass right through material substances. Neither could they communicate verbally with people still in their natural bodies.

Many watched doctors work on their physical bodies while they floated above. They were free of pain until they re-entered the natural body. Other saints, finding themselves in the spiritual realm, viewed angels as well as demons. Numerous books tell of these experiences. Although these experiences have probably been happening all along, until recently most people were probably reluctant to share them, lest they not be believed.

Witches and psychics travel about in their spirit bodies. It's portrayed on Halloween as a witch on a broomstick. Eastern yogi adepts also travel outside the natural body. This practice is taught by demons. It gives the yogi, or witches, power. They can travel anywhere and be as "a fly on the wall" observing everything without revealing their presence.

God forbids the practice because of the evil that can result. Besides that, it is very dangerous, because the spirit is open to attack from very wicked spirits, who can prevent the return to the body, bringing death.

These same unholy spirits can access our spirits, even when in the body, if it is unprotected by righteousness.

Proverbs says, "He that hath no rule over his own spirit is like a city that is broken down and without walls" (Proverbs 25:28). A city without walls lies vulnerable to invasion. Walls are built to keep something out or in. Speaking about Israel's future Isaiah says a song will be sung: "We have a strong city; salvation will God appoint for walls and bulwark" (Isaiah 26:1). And again in chapter 60 he says of Israel, "thou shalt call thy walls Salvation and thy gates Praise" (vs.18). Calling walls salvation is consistent with spiritual truth. Complete protection from the spirit world lies in salvation and righteousness. The natural man is open to attack from the spirit world the minute he loses his innocence and delves into sin. Before salvation men are said to be "dead in trespasses and sin" (Ephesians. 2:1). Sin attracts unclean spirits.

Continual practice of sin breaks down walls, and spirit entities plunder at will. When they set up strongholds in the spirit, they interfere with behavior and compete with the man for the direction of his own soul through the will. The Bible speaks of such as demonized. Jesus set many free from their influence when he ministered on earth. The amount of control over a man depends upon the amount of cooperation, or agreement he has given the demons, by participating with them in sin.

Paul admonished the Corinthians, "Having therefore these promises [that God would dwell in them and walk with them], dearly beloved, let us cleanse ourselves from all filthiness of the flesh and spirit perfecting holiness in the fear of God" (2 Corinthians 7:1). So according to Paul, the spirit also can be dirtied with sin, which is contrary to most doctrine taught today. But we must remember the spirit is a communicator with the spirit world. Contact with unclean spirits brings defilement.

For this reason the spirit body needs the protection of the whole armor of God. The first defense is truth. So surround yourself with a girdle of truth, because all dark powers operate with deception. Thus, truth protects.

The next piece of armor is the breastplate of righteousness. A pure heart repels unclean spirits. Jesus said, ". . . the prince of this world cometh, and hath nothing in me" (John 15:31). Satan moved against Jesus by the evil he inspired in wicked men. That was the only way he could touch Him. And that is the only way Satan can touch us if we keep a pure heart. The shoes of peace represent a rest brought about by obedient service, entering into God's rest (Heb.4:5, 6). A soldier stands still until ordered to march. Through this rest, rebellious and self-exalting motivations may be resisted. Great peace comes from knowing we are in God's perfect will. In this way the gospel goes forth in God's time and will be completely successful.

Next, the sure knowledge that God will take care of us, regardless of the enemy's attack, becomes a shield of faith. Here we trust wholly in God and put no trust in men.

After that, the helmet of salvation fits over our spiritual head, protecting the soul's mind from discouragement and fear. It also becomes a bulwark against doubt, protecting the believer's assurance of salvation.

The sword of the spirit, the only part of the armor designed for offense as well as defense, protects and reproaches the enemy causing danger by giving a directive word to us. The Holy Spirit speaks his Word to our intuition directly. By this we receive supernatural instruction for the battle. We fight back with this specific Word from the Spirit for that particular incident and see God's power manifest. It will be a pointed thrust to destroy Satan's strategy.

The seventh and last weapon against the spirit world is *all* prayer inspired by the Holy Spirit in accord with God's will. Sometimes this means praying supernaturally in a tongue[2] we have never learned. When we yield our tongue to the Holy Spirit, God enables our tongue to pray for things our mind knows nothing about. In prayer, we call for spiritual help, and we give God an avenue to help us or others with specific help. It also builds up the power of the Spirit in us. When rebuking the Corinthian church for the misuse of this gift, Paul said, "I thank my God, that I speak in tongues more than ye all" (1 Corinthians 14:18 AV). Yet we never read of him speaking in tongues in public. I wonder if this was the secret of God's mighty power working through Paul.

We have digressed far from our subject of the armor of God for the spirit body. Nevertheless, the gift of tongues is a mighty gift for strengthening the new man. Getting back now to the armor, when we understand why we need the whole armor, it is much easier to obey the command. Paul says it several ways. Keep yourselves in the love of God. Put on the Lord Jesus Christ. He also says, "let us cast off the works of darkness, and let us put on the armor of light" (Romans 13:12). Righteousness appears as light in the spiritual world. Reflecting the glory of God in righteousness repels spirits of darkness. When we obey these

---

[2] This is one of the power gifts of the Holy Spirit. It's a real language not gibberish as some suppose, a gift meant to be used mainly in the prayer closet. It can be used as praise or intercessory prayer.

admonitions, we clear the way for God's Spirit to dwell in us in fullness.

Conclusion

Contrary to what many teach, the spirit is not some inner sanctum where only God can dwell. Rather, the spirit is the very life, energy, and operating power of a man. It has input and output channels the same as the body and communicates with the spirit world just like the body communicates with the natural world. In fact, the spirit has its own body with which to communicate. It can be sullied by contact with unclean spirits and is buried under sin in the natural man. Because of sin, spirits have access to the spirit and can bring various degrees of bondage. Also because of sin, the Word commands Christians to put
on the whole armor of God and walk in the light, so that God may direct their lives unhindered.

3

Made in His Image

> And God said, Let us make man in our image, after our likeness: and let them have dominion over the fish of the sea, and over the birds of the heavens, and over the cattle, and over all the earth, and over every creeping thing that creepeth upon the earth.
>
> And God created man in his own image, in the image of God created he him; male and female created he them.
>
> **Genesis 1:26, 27AV**

Adam was made in the image of God. Being the descendants of Adam, we also have his image. Of course, we've been greatly changed by the marring of sin. Nevertheless, we may still have the same basic structure. We know that we are like God, because even in the Old Testament, when Jesus appeared as the angel of the Lord, He took the form of a man. We could say that this is the meaning of the Scripture above. Man simply has the same form in which God chooses to reveal Himself.

We have a command center (our soul), a communicator with the material world (our body), and a communicator with the spirit world (our spirit). God has a command center (the Father), a communicator with the material world (the Son), and a communicator with the spiritual world (the Holy Spirit). He has three persons who cooperate with one another perfectly. Each one dwells in equal majesty with the other, yet the Father is said to be greater than the Son (John 10:14, 29). His greatness appears to be because He decides everything. Both the Son and the Spirit obey the Father's will.

When Jesus was in the flesh the Spirit drove the Son into the wilderness to be tested. At that instance, the Father's command came through the Spirit. But after the Son was glorified, he asked the Father to send the Spirit to his disciples as a gift. So the Spirit and the Son can direct each other according to the will of the Father. During his ministry on earth, Jesus was present with his disciples in the material world, but his communication with them was limited to their understanding. By sending his Spirit after His ascension, He communicated directly with them through His Holy Spirit making them to understand the things of God, because *now* he could communicate directly with their spirits.

When we understand our tri-part being functions, we begin to understand, *in a small way*, the functions of the Godhead. The Father compares to our soul, which has mind, will and emotions. The following is an attempt to diagram this showing the action of His soul.[3] In several Old Testament Scriptures God refers to His own soul. He even refers to His heart in Psalm 33:11: "The counsel of the Lord standeth for ever, and the thoughts of his heart to all generations." And Yea, I will rejoice over them to do good, and

---

3 Scriptures featuring God's soul: Lev.26:11, 30; Ps. 11:5; Isa. 1:14, 42:1; Jer. 5:29, 6:8; Zech. 11:8

I will plant them in this land assuredly with my whole heart and with my whole soul (Jeremiah 32:41AV).

FATHER—Acting as the Soul of God

Reveals (Matthew 16:17)	Mind
Formulate plans (Matthew 25:34)	
Knows (Matthew 6:32; Luke2:30	
Seeks (John 4:24)	Will
Promises (Luke 24:49)	
Decides times (Matthew 24:36)	
Appoints (Luke 22:29)	
Wishes (Luke 22:42; John 6:39)	
Seals (John 6:27)	
Gives honors (John 6:32; 13:3)	
Delivers to tormentors (Matthew 18:34, 35)	
Glorifies (John 17:1)	
Sends angels (Matthew 26:53)	
Sends men (John 5:23, 30, 36)	
Raises the dead (John 5:21)	
Works (John 5:17)	
Reveals (Matthew 16:17)	
Formulates plans (Matthew25:34)	
Loves (John 3:16, 35)	Emotions
Delights (Prov. 8:27-32)	
Forgives (Matthew 6:14, 15; Mark 11:26)	
Angry with the Wicked (Ps 7:11)	
Jealous Exodus 34:14)	

He also fathers spirits (Hebrews 12:9), lights (James 1:17), and the believers in Christ (Colossians. 1:2). The Father plans everything. He is the source of everything. He sits on a throne (Revelation 3:21) and rules over all.

The Son is the body of God, Colossians 1:15 says Christ is "the image of the invisible God, the firstborn of all creation;" and ". . . For in him [that is Christ] dwelleth the fullness of the Godhead bodily" (Colossians 2:9)

Some Old Testament appearances of God in the image of a man are:

Captain of the Lord's Army (Joshua 5:14, 15)
Son of man in fiery furnace (Daniel 3:25)
Man on chariot throne (Ezekiel 1:26)
Son of man to rule (Daniel 7:13, 14)

And since the Son is the Father's contact with the material world, through the Son, he created the heavens and the earth (Hebrews 1:1, 2). Although the Father's mind was the architect, the Son created it according to the plans like a contractor. Through the Son the Father reveals himself to man (Hebrews. 1:1-3). Since God is a spiritual being and invisible to the physical world, he took a form that could be seen by mortal men (Colossians 2:9).

Thus, communication with the natural world comes through the Son or through angels (messengers) manifesting temporarily in material form according to Judges 13:16-21. Jesus came to glorify the Father, speak the Father's words and do the Father's work. The Father was in Jesus when He dwelt on earth, because when Phillip asked the Lord to reveal the Father, He said, "He who has seen me has seen the Father" (John 14:9).

Jesus was in the Father and the Father was in Him, just as we are in our souls and our souls are in us. (But unlike us, the Father was on the throne in heaven as well.) Using a computer as an example again, the Father is like the mainframe computer in a network. The Son is like a terminal outlet, which has instant access to everything in the main frame, but is located in a different location. Jesus' many analogies comparing Him with the material world may be another indication that he represents the Godhead's communication with the created world. For instance, he referred to himself as the bread from heaven (John 6:33-35) and the light of the world (John 8:12). John introduced him as the word of life (John 1:1), that is, God's expression in this world and later said, "We have seen and our hands have handled the word of life." The writer of the book of Hebrews (Heb. 1:3) called him the express image of God, the brightness of God's glory, the effulgence (the manifestation of energy in a material world).

In the Godhead, only Jesus is visible to the material world. In this sense, the Son compares with our body, our communicator with the material world. For this reason, the Father planned for the Son to have a material body in which He could both communicate with His creatures and redeem them legally; i.e., be of the same type of body so he could be a substitute sacrifice (Hebrews. 2:14). If man were not made in the image of God, Jesus could not be an exact substitute.

The Exchange of Souls

Understanding Jesus' exact image of us, throws further light on the act of redemption. When Jesus' body was on the cross, the soul of God (Psalm 11:5 speaks of the soul of God), the Father, departed. Then He replaced himself in Christ with the sinful thoughts and the collective fouled consciences of all mankind for all time.

In other words, the collective sin-sick souls of earth became his soul, when He "was made sin for us" (2 Corinthians 5:21). The Father's infinite nature being removed left room for any number of finite souls to be placed in Christ.

Thus, it can be said that Jesus died for the whole world (1 John 2:2) when he suffered for mankind.

He had a natural body from this earth, but the eternal, immortal and omnipotent Holy Spirit supplied his vitality. So the life that he gave was infinite. That is why he was able to receive the collective souls of mankind, them being finite, a countable number.

Therefore, he was a complete substitute in the judgment of death. His holy nature took on the sins of us all and endured them in six hours on the cross. (Six is the spiritual number in Scripture connected to both man and sin.) What agony Jesus must have felt when He was made sin for us! Just anticipating it made him sweat great drops of blood. No wonder then that he cried out:

> **My God; My God, why hast thou forsaken me? Why art thou so far from helping me, and from the words of my roaring? O my God, I cry in the daytime, but thou hearest not; and in the night season, and am not silent. But thou art holy . . . [that's why]. Psalm 22:1-3aAV**

Being made sin shut the Father off from the Son because of holiness. The Holy Spirit did not leave Him, however, for again the Scripture says, "How much more shall the blood of Christ, who *through* the eternal Spirit offered himself without spot to God, purge your *conscience* from dead works to serve the living God" (Hebrews. 9:14). So the Spirit also suffered in the judgment laid upon Christ. He became buried under sin like the consciences in the spirits of sinful men.

Then, after the suffering was complete, Jesus dismissed His life in the flesh and sent His spirit body, totally empowered by the Holy Spirit, into hell where he took the captives captive and preached unto the spirits in prison (1 Peter 3:19-21). The presence of the Holy Spirit was necessary to clear the consciences of men and to raise Jesus out of hell's depths with a dazzling display of power.

When believers sink below the water in baptism, they personally identify with His death and punishment, and this realization enables them to be free from all guilt, thus cleansing their consciences. When they go into the water, they symbolize Christ going into death, and consequently hell. When they come out of the water, they symbolize Christ's resurrection, rising up in mighty power. Identifying with Christ's death, they see their sins entirely paid for, clearing their conscience of sin against God.

The Cleansed Conscience

Hebrews 9:9 contends that animal sacrifices had to be repeated over and over, because they could not clear the conscience,: ". . . for the time then present, in which were offered both gifts and sacrifices, that did not make him that did the service perfect, as pertaining to the conscience." Since the conscience is a spiritual function, only a spiritual being could redeem it. Animals possess mere vitalizing spirits with no other function than to give life and emotional expression. Speaking in other words, they have no conscience. So how could they atone for the spiritual? The writer of Hebrews repeats the same argument:

> For the law having a shadow of the good things to come, not the very image of the things, can never with the same sacrifices year by year, which they offer continually, make perfect them that draw nigh. Else would they not have ceased to be offered? because the worshippers, having been once cleansed, would have had

no more consciousness of sins. But in those sacrifices there is a remembrance made of sins year by year.

Hebrews 10:1-3 NKJV

The Holy Spirit is the spirit body of God and His power in both the spiritual and natural worlds. Mary conceived the spirit (life vitality) of Christ by the Holy Spirit. Thirty years later the Father bestowed the Spirit upon Christ without measure as the "anointed one" following Jesus' water baptism.

The Holy Spirit, who descended upon him in the form of dove (Luke 3:22), clearly came from the Father for he immediately said, "Thou art my beloved son; in whom I am well pleased." On that day, Jesus, the man, became Jesus, the Christ, the anointed one. This picture exemplifies how believers are further baptized in the Spirit following baptism in water. But first they are born again when new life from God enters their spirits at the moment of faith. After that they are baptized in water identifying with Christ's death and the clearing of their consciences.

After Christ's death Peter says He preached to the spirits in prison (hell) who had lived just before the flood, during the time when Noah prepared the ark. These had to be among the wickedest men who ever lived and therefore, were probably kept in the lowest level of hell. His preaching to them was probably similar to the preaching of Father Abraham to the rich man in hell, reminding each that he deserved his fate. But the point that Peter makes is that Christ carried our sins into the lowest hell, paying the ultimate price, so that we, or even the most evil of sinners who accepted Christ, could have a clear conscience by knowing every sin was paid for in full.

He preached to these spirits while His physical body lay in the grave. Thus, his Spirit body (because of the Holy Spirit), possessing omnipotent power, overthrew the forces of hell, defeating forever God's adversary, Satan. When Jesus arose from the grave, His indestructible new body had taken on certain characteristics that were visible in the natural world. In His new body He was able to materialize or de-materialize at will even walk through doors. This body also rose visibly into the clouds in defiance of gravity.

The Comforter Comes

When Jesus returned to Heaven, the Father sent the Holy Spirit to earth to minister through believers. Because He is spirit, demons can see Him. They tremble because of His mighty power. His power residing in believers defeats demons. His Spirit body occupies their spirit bodies to the measure that they are emptied for Him. His word commands believers to be filled with the Holy Spirit (Ephesians 5:18). He communicates with them and demonstrates the power of God to them through the spiritual realm. The initial filling comes when baptized in the Spirit (separate from water baptism). Here they are anointed with His power for service in ministry, giving access to the power gifts mentioned in the chapter on the spirit. Subsequent fillings become the responsibility of the believer to obey the command to "be filled with the Spirit" (Ephesians 5:18).

During a worship service the Holy Spirit manifests Himself among believers collectively. If they are spiritually keen, they can sense His presence. They recognize the anointing of His presence upon those ministering worship. They also feel the bond of the body of Christ and the Spirit uniting in communion.

Becoming Like Him

Yes, we are made in God's image; therefore, we are likeHim in a miniscule way. He also has a command center, the Father; a material world communicator, the Son; and a spiritual world communicator, the Holy Spirit. We have a command center, the soul; a material world communicator, the body; and a spiritual world communicator, the spirit. *But this is where the likeness ends!*

God dwells primarily in the spiritual realm. Jesus told the woman at the well, "God is a spirit . . .," while we were created to dwell in the material world. The difference between the two worlds lies in their make-up.

The physical worlds consist of molecules, electrons and such of the basic elements of the universe as are found in terrestrial bodies. Here the exchange of matter and energy operates at a slower pace than in celestial bodies, which are electrical dynamos of energy. Paul uses the contrast of the two to explain the resurrection 1 Corinthians. 15).

From this contrast we could deduce that the spiritual realm is a world of pure energy, operating in what scientists call plasma. The "eternal, immortal, invisible God" is without doubt an immense dynamo of energy, greater than millions and millions of suns.

The first law of physics states that matter is neither created nor destroyed but merely changes form, passing from energy to matter and vice versa. Plasmas, said to make up 99.9% of the universe, are nothing more than constituent parts of ionized atoms with some of their electrons missing. Together they make a kind of primordial soup made up of unfinished molecules from which God makes all things.

God was the first cause, the creator, and His first creation was a congregation of spiritual beings called the "sons of God" or angels. These angels He created from His vast stores of energy. He made them to exist forever (Revelation 20:10). Paul says in 1 Corinthians. 8:6, "Yet for us there is but one God, the Father, from whom all things came . . ."

Adam's race differs from the angels in that they dwell in a temporary material world; temporary, because it is in a constant state of change. God devised a plan, even before He laid the foundations of the earth. He decided to create a material world and populate it with physical mankind. Knowing Satan would try to destroy His latest creation, He commissioned the Son to become a man and through his manhood raise mankind up to a ruling position through redemption. Thus, he would defeat and dethrone Satan and his rebellious angels. (Satan claims authority as the Prince of the power of the air.) God the Father said to Jesus, "You are my son; today I have become your Father" (Psalms 2:7).

He created the angels first, because the writer to the Hebrews declares, "For to which of the angels did God ever say, You are my son, today I have become your Father?" (Heb. 5:5). At the same time He intended to create a new spiritual congregation, more intimate than angels, a spiritual *family*, who would eventually rule in place of Satan and his angels.

Though mankind is not like God in that they are of the earth, and temporary, they are, however, destined *to become like Him through the redemption process.* Jesus, the man, became a sort of hybrid after his resurrection. He was able for the first time to dwell equally in the material and spiritual worlds. (His appearances in the shape of a man in the Old Testament were temporary, probably not his natural state.) Believers shall have bodies like His new resurrection body, which shall also make them at home in both worlds.

It is nothing for God to change their bodies and their spirits to the spiritual mode. Their bodies simply become a different kind of flesh according to His purposes. Their spirits already possess the properties to function in the spirit world, either with God or without Him—in heaven or in the lake of fire. But the matter of the soul differs entirely. A soul develops according to its mode. God, in His sovereignty gave mankind a free will in this matter. He also gave believers all the resources to become like Him. That means any changes that take place in the soul, must be made by the person himself. If a believer's command center insists on operating in the fleshly mode, he may ultimately be like God in bodily resurrection, but not like Him in character. Nobody truly resembles God unless he also has His character.

Paul's goal for his converts was to be conformed to the image of Christ. This process, called sanctification, redeems the soul. Sanctification takes place over a lifetime. From the minute that believers are born again by the Spirit of God until the day they die, their souls should be changing into the image of Christ. I say "should be," because the matter rests solely in each one's will. If he chooses to walk in the Spirit instead of in the flesh, he will be constantly changing. The Scripture says as believers behold His image in the Word, they shall be changed into that same image (2 Corinthians. 3:18AV).

But when they choose to walk in the flesh, no change takes place. Jesus came, not only to die for mankind, but also to show them how to live. His example, in the gospels and the teaching of the laws governing righteousness, helps each one to change to be like Him. When mankind learns how to obey the new laws, they begin to change. Only then will the *kingdom rule of God* be visible *in* believers.

SECTION TWO
Attitudes and Laws

Attitudes - Plus the Laws

In the Sermon on the Mount, Jesus taught his disciples how to conduct themselves by living under the laws of the kingdom. By using these laws as guidelines, Christians learn how to walk in the Spirit and begin to develop the characteristics of God.

Importance of Attitude

I once heard a preacher say, "The only thing in your life you really have control over is your attitude." What I think he meant was that we make choices about how we will meet the challenges of life. We let circumstances overwhelm us, or we determine to meet them with the will to overcome them. Jesus' instruction majored on areas that bring the greatest challenges to life. Jesus preceded the nine laws of the kingdom found in Matthew chapters five, six, and seven with what we call the "Beatitudes," of which there are also nine. If our attitudes toward these are focused aright and we obey his commandments, the end result will be righteousness, holiness, and peace.

Jesus began at the heart level. Because it is the soul that needs changing, particularly its heart, and since the heart drives the will of a man, the heart is the logical place to start. However, knowing what is right and being disposed to do it are two different things. Attitude always precedes action. First, get the attitude right, and then obey the law associated with it.

Webster's New World Dictionary defines "attitude" thus: 1. a bodily posture showing mood, action, etc. 2. a manner showing one's feelings or thoughts.

Remember, the spirit is the part of us that charges our emotions and energizes our moods. Therefore, the Beatitudes address man's spirit and the laws address man's soul. (Laws have to do with direction, which leads to action. Consequently, the will to act upon them is an action of the soul.)

The "be" attitudes have a focus toward something. So our first task will be to uncover that "something." Later we will be able to match each attitude with a law. When these attitudes and laws work together, they produce one of the nine fruits of the Spirit, hence the importance of obeying his commandments.

Let us look at the first attitude:

(1) "Blessed are the poor in spirit: for theirs is the kingdom of heaven."

Isaiah 57:15 tells us that God dwells in the high and holy place and with him also that is of a contrite and humble spirit. The humble spirit belongs to the kingdom of heaven and the kingdom of heaven belongs to him, because he submits willingly to the rule from above. Therefore, humility characterizes this attitude. "Poor in spirit" describes our proper attitude toward God. Being rich in our own spirit describes a proud heart. Both James (James 4:6) and Peter (1 Peter 5:5) say that God resists the proud but gives grace to the humble. Nothing is available to the believer without grace; so in all our dealings with God, whether in prayer, or in service of any kind, our attitude toward God must always be one of humility. Otherwise nothing spiritual will happen!

(2) "Blessed are they that mourn: for they shall be comforted."

Mourning is the attitude we should develop toward sin. Forgiveness comes after repentance and with it comes comfort, a release from the conscience. But without a mourning attitude, we would never repent. A tolerance for sin prevents righteousness and holiness. If we compromise just slightly in the beginning, gradually we will become more and more tolerant until sin rules our lives. As long as our attitude allows for some sin, we cannot be righteous. One drop of contamination renders any substance impure. Being satisfied with some sin in our lives prevents cleansing, because we have no desire to change (repent).

Paul told Timothy that "the love of money is the root of all evil" (1 Timothy. 4:10 AV), so we can expect that developing the right attitude toward sin will involve money. Thus, having the proper attitude toward money and a grieving attitude toward sin is a prerequisite for righteousness.

(3)"Blessed are the meek: for they shall inherit the earth."

Meekness is the attitude we should develop toward offenses. Not being a milquetoast or "softie," meekness is the same word the Greeks used to describe their high-spirited, yet highly trained war horses. Though they had great strength, they remained under control because of their training. In the same way meekness can be defined as "controlled strength."

It is easy to see why meekness would be an asset when faced with an offense. The natural response would be anger. Thus, meekness is a supernatural trait for us to develop. The meek shall inherit the earth because they will survive the judgment of wicked men (Psalm 37:9-11; Psalm 76:9). Of course, another fulfillment of that verse could be the meek are fit to reign over the earth, since they are always under control.

(4) "Blessed are they that hunger and thirst after righteousness: for they shall be filled."

Hungering and thirsting is the attitude we need toward the Word of God. The Bible shows us how to live and what God expects from his people. All spiritual growth, including the fruits of righteousness, comes from understanding the Scriptures. Any earnest seeker will receive satisfaction and fulfillment from his searching of God's Word.

Hunger and thirst answer to the Word as the bread and water of life. Eating the bread of life corresponds to the "logos" (Greek for Word), which refers to receiving the life of Jesus for growth and maturity from reading the Word and hearing it taught. The water of life refers to a specific spoken Word, or "rhema" (different Greek "word" for Word), where the Holy Spirit speaks directly to one's spirit for enlightenment or direction.

Without a hunger and thirst for the Word, the spiritual life dries up, and joy departs. Without hunger and thirst, we will never understand how to handle the pitfalls of life. Since walking as Jesus walked is our goal, we need to hunger and thirst after the things of God, particularly his Word.

(5) "Blessed are the merciful: for they shall obtain mercy.

Mercy is the attitude we should have toward all others. A merciful person recognizes his own imperfection and makes allowances for others accordingly. God shows mercy to us. Psalm 103:13, 14 NKJV says: "As a father pities his children, So the LORD pities those who fear Him. For He knows our frame; He remembers that we are dust." He recognizes our weaknesses and shows mercy. With-out this attitude, we would be under constant judgment.

We need to watch out for forming strong attitudes of condemnation toward our fellow human beings for various weaknesses we observe in them. If we show mercy toward their weaknesses, they will be more apt to do the same for us, because our reaction to others is usually a reaction to *their attitudes*. Satan is the accuser of the brethren; Jesus is our advocate who stands in the gap. We will imitate one or the other. When we criticize, we become accusers of our brethren. When we pray for them because we see a "gap" between what they are and what they should be, we become like Jesus. In praying for them, we emulate what Jesus does for us (Hebrews 7:24, 25). All our brothers need mercy, mercy, mercy!

(6) "Blessed are the pure in heart: for they shall see God."

Purity is the attitude we need to have concerning ourselves. Although we should show mercy to others for their weaknesses, we must keep strict moral limitations on ourselves. A pure heart keeps a clear conscience by avoiding sinful acts.

Purity, a prerequisite to holiness, prepares us for the presence of God, the place where He reveals Himself (1 John 3:6; 3 John 9-11). Only the pure in heart can "see" God. The word for "see" in this passage means, "to gaze upon with wonder." The pure are able to marvel at the glorious character of God in all His splendor, because they are striving for purity that is pleasing to Him. Habakkuk says of the Lord, "You are of purer eyes than to behold evil, and cannot look on wickedness" (1:13). "Behold" here could be translated "show self to." "Look" could be translated to "look intently at" (for deriving pleasure). These Scriptures surely imply that God takes pleasure in the pure of heart and reveals Himself to them, but he does not reveal Himself to or take pleasure in the wicked.

(7) "Blessed are the peacemakers: for they shall be called the children of God."

The attitude of peacemaking is one that is directed toward the kingdom of God and his authority. We become like him when we obey his Word, and we imitate him when we *keep our word*. A broken law, a broken covenant, or a broken word causes most peace-disturbing incidents, whether our word is given to God or to our fellow men. War erupts between the parties involved because of disappointed expectations. When we learn to abide in peace and endeavor to keep the peace, we are called "the children of God," because peace is the hallmark of his Kingdom.

He keeps the peace because he keeps his Word. A human father maintains discipline and proper behavior in his children by first setting bounds and warning of consequences when those bounds are over-run. If he keeps his word regarding the punishment for disobedience, the children soon learn to abide within the bounds—keeping peace in the household.

God the Father rules his household the same way. The God of peace is one of his titles. A peacemaker, or as we call it, a peace officer, is one in authority. Several times in the New Testament the writers ascribe this title to God. Romans 16:20 mentions that the God of peace will soon crush Satan under the believer's feet, which speaks of his authority to do that. In Philippians 4:9 Paul admonishes the Philippians to obey the instructions he gave them; and the God of Peace would be with them. Here they were to obey what teachings God had given Paul, again showing God's authority over life.

1 Thessalonians 5:23 speaks of the same thing: "Now may the *God of peace* Himself sanctify you completely; and may your whole spirit, soul, and body be preserved blameless at the coming of our Lord Jesus Christ." The God of Peace is with us and sanctifies us and preserves us blameless when we submit to his authority and keep his Word. When we walk in His ways, the peace of God dwells within. We also walk in reverential fear of God because of his authority.

(8) "Blessed are those who are persecuted for righteousness' sake, For theirs is the kingdom of heaven."

This attitude just naturally follows the former one. If we recognize the supreme authority of God, then we also recognize that we should do what is right no matter what the circumstances. There is no guarantee, however, that the world will treat us right. In fact, it is an invitation for the world, whose standards we may expose as wicked, to persecute *us*.

This is the attitude we develop toward suffering. We did what was right, but the world made us suffer for it. "It's not fair," we may complain. But Jesus said, "In the world you will have tribulation, but be of good cheer, I have overcome the world" (John 16:33).

No, the world does not play fair, but it is better to suffer as Jesus did than to try and get even. It pleases God when we suffer for doing right. As Peter said, "But and if ye suffer for righteousness' sake, happy are ye . . . Having a good conscience; that, whereas they speak evil of you, as of evildoers, they may be ashamed that falsely accuse your good conversation (Peter 3:14, 16).

9) "Blessed are you when they revile and persecute you, and say all kinds of evil against you falsely for My sake. Rejoice and be exceedingly glad, for great is your reward in heaven, for so they persecuted the prophets who were before you."

Being persecuted for Jesus' sake only occurs when we make a dent in Satan's territory because of being totally in God's will. Therefore, we can rejoice in our successful service to the Lord. Jesus said, "Woe you when all men spoke well of you!" (Luke 6:26, 27). If all men approve of you there must be compromise in your life.

Rejoicing in persecution is the attitude to have toward enemies. True enemies of a committed Christian are the enemies of the Lord: Satan and his minions. Therefore, it is they who manipulate those who come against believers, duping or deceiving them. When we can recognize the enemy behind the person, we can show the love of Christ to those so used, our human enemy. It is highly pleasing to the Lord to have His attitude toward his enemies. He prayed, "Father forgive them, for they know not what they do," even as they nailed him to the cross.

Summarizing the focus of the "be" attitudes, we find the following:

1. Humility = attitude toward God
2. Mourning = attitude toward Sin
3. Meekness = attitude toward offenses
4. Hunger and Thirst = attitude toward the Word of God
5. Mercy = attitude toward Others
6. Peacekeeping = attitude toward the Authority of God
7. Purity = attitude toward one's Self
8. Endurance = attitude toward Suffering (for doing right)
9. Rejoicing = attitude toward Suffering (from enemies)

If we can get our attitudes right, we are taking the first step toward developing the fruits of the Spirit.

We cannot pass by the attitudes without realizing the root causes of problems that are affected by them. The writer to the Hebrews states three reasons for the grace of

God to fail in our lives: temporal values, immorality, and bitterness (Hebrews 12:15). (It may be from here that Bill Gothard, the seminar speaker on Basic Youth Conflicts, took his three root causes.) Comparing them with our attitudes, we can see that we have three for each root problem. If we have the proper attitude toward God, the word of God, and the authority of God, we will not be troubled by problems relating to temporal values.

If we have the proper attitude toward sin, self and others will not be tempted toward immorality. And finally, if we have the proper attitude toward offenses, suffering, and enemies, we will not be eaten up with bitterness. Looking at it graphically, we can see the relationship between the root causes and the proper attitudes:

Diagram of Attitudes Relating to Root Causes

Temporal Values	Immorality	Bitterness
God	Sin	Offenses
Word of God	Self	Suffering
Authority of God	Others	Enemies

These attitudes cover every dimension of life.

Light and Salt

Jesus concluded His lesson on attitudes by telling His students that they were to be the salt of the world. By this statement He meant that by holding these attitudes, they would show the world the proper way to live. They would also reprove the world of its wickedness and thus hinder its freedom to sin. In the long run it would preserve the world from God's judgment. But if the salt failed to be salt, the world would spoil causing God's judgment to fall.

Jesus also told them they would be the light of the world. It is interesting that he mentioned putting a light on a candlestick for all in the house (our houses) to see (Matthew 6:15). By looking at the way we live at home, men see the real person. If we keep the be-attitudes at home then we will also keep them at work (our bushels).

The bushel also represents a measure, which had to do with commerce in Jesus' day. That is why I say it represents us in our place of employment. But it is also a container. Placing a container over our lights would not prevent light from shining, it would only limit it. I think what Jesus was saying was this: Let your light shine without any limitations; first at home and then at work. Be real in both places. When we do, we show the world how to live

Laws that Govern Righteous Behavior

Having introduced the proper attitudes, Jesus turns to the laws themselves. Yet before He declares the first law, He takes time to express their importance. He explains:

> **Do not think that I came to destroy the Law or the Prophets. I did not come to destroy but to fulfill. For assuredly, I say to you, till heaven and earth pass away, one jot or one title will by no means pass from the law till all is fulfilled. Whoever therefore breaks one of the least of these commandments, and teaches men so, shall be called least in the kingdom of heaven; but whoever does and teaches them, he shall be called great in the kingdom of heaven. For I say to you, that unless your righteousness exceeds the righteousness of the scribes and Pharisees, you will by no means** *enter the kingdom of heaven.*
>
> Matthew 5:17-20 NKJV (Emphasis added)

All the laws of God stand and have their purpose. Much of the ceremonial law was fulfilled in Jesus' death. That is why the Church does not obey them. But not the laws governing proper behavior, they were simply superseded with a greater righteousness. The laws that follow are the "these" Jesus referred to. They go beyond the Ten Commandments. They are the nine commandments of righteousness. The keeping of "these" makes one great in the kingdom.

The keeping of the additions of the Talmud (up to the time of Jesus) were just the keeping of a set of rules. God was about to terminate the Old Covenant, along with its blood sacrifices, and replace it with the New Covenant. Thus, the traditions added to the law were outside of the kingdom of God.

These laws became a stumbling block to the Jews. That is why Jesus said, "Except your righteousness exceed that of the scribes and Pharisees ye shall in no case enter the kingdom of heaven." To be under the authority of God, one must obey the rules He decrees.

First, one must be able to see that the kingdom exists *and* that His new laws supersede the keeping of the old, because Christ has brought a "new and living way" (Hebrews 19:20). Jesus told Nicodemus that except a man be born again, he cannot *see* the kingdom of God. But knowing it exists and entering it are two different things. Living in the flesh excludes the kingdom of God, for Romans 8:7 tells us that the carnal (fleshly) mind is not subject to the law of God. So entering the kingdom of God means living in the Spirit in accordance with the principles and laws of righteousness which He instituted in the Sermon on the Mount.

The Laws in General

The laws of God are like a hedge or a fence to keep out marauding spirits and protect those who remain within their walls. All of the Ten Commandments, when broken, invite demonic activity into the life. That is why an offender had to be put to death. Before Jesus came, there was no remedy for demonic invasion. It is also the reason why Jesus said that He came not to destroy (disintegrate) the law, because that would expose mankind to the demon hoard. Rather, he came to fulfill—"cram, level, verify or finish"—the law. In other words, He came to fill in the cracks in the wall and perfect those who were obedient into righteous beings. He further said that not one tiny letter of the law and not one single punctuation mark would be left out, until all be fulfilled. The word for "fulfilled" here means to parcel out as a prescription. Therefore, we could say that the Laws of the Kingdom are a prescription from God to cure the flesh and make us spiritually healthy.

The end-result of keeping these laws produces an armor consisting of moral uprightness imitating Christ's, which manifests itself in the spirit world as light. Paul says in Romans 13 that to put on the Lord Jesus Christ is to put on an armor of light. Wickedness cannot stand in the light, but will flee from it. Matthew 13:43 speaks of righteous believers shining as the sun in the kingdom of their Father.

In the next few chapters we will look at these laws individually. These are not mere suggestions. After all, Jesus Himself called them commandments. He even prefaced these laws by saying, "Whosoever therefore shall break one of these least commandments, and shall teach men so, he shall be called the least in the kingdom of heaven:" If corrupting the teaching of these laws affects the teacher's position in the kingdom, they must be extremely important to the sanctification of all our souls, even to the point of determining our position in the kingdom rule.

Here we introduce them as a whole and give the fruit connected to them, that you might realize how truly important they are *to you*. For this reason I will often address you personally as we look at them together.

I. The Law of Anger: A law that governs the control of anger, when applied with the proper attitude toward offenses, develops meekness.

II. The Law of Purity: A law that governs personal morality, when applied with the proper attitude toward self, develops goodness.

III. The Law of Fidelity: A law that governs keeping your word, when applied with the proper attitude toward God's authority, develops peace.

IV. The Law of Flexibility: A law that governs the desire for "getting even" for suffering injustice. When applied toward suffering with the proper attitude, develops gentleness.

V. The Law of Impartiality: A Law that governs our attitudes and actions toward those who oppose us, when applied toward enemies, develops "agape" love.

VI. The Law of Devotion: A law that governs our relationship with the Father, when applied with the proper attitude toward devotion to God, develops faithfulness as well as faith.

VII. The Law of Acquisition: A law that governs our acquisition and attitude toward money and substance, which when properly applied, curbs lusts and develops temperance or self-control.

VIII. The Law of Criticism: A law that governs our assessment in observation of others, and their abilities, which when properly applied, develops long-suffering or patience with the weaknesses of others.

IX. The Law of Understanding: A Law that governs how to conduct one's self inside the kingdom of God, which when applied with proper attitude, develops joy.

Irritation Versus Placation: The Law of Anger

Jesus began His discourse on anger by reminding the disciples of the Old Testament Law. Citing murder as the worst possible response to an offense, He says,

> Ye have heard that it was said to them of old time, Thou shalt not kill; and whosoever shall kill shall be in danger of the judgment: *but I say unto you*, that every one who is angry with his brother without a cause shall be in danger of the judgment; and whosoever shall say to his brother, Raca, shall be in danger of the council; and whosoever shall say, Thou fool, shall be in danger of the hell fire.
>
> Matthew 5:21, 22 AV (Emphasis added)

Anger begins small, but left unchecked can grow to great proportions. Jesus goes straight to the heart where anger begins. When I am angry with my brother without cause, it is probably some small irritation with how he acts, dresses, or some shortcoming in his personality. This small attitude of anger builds a frame of reference. Each time the brother irritates me, it accumulates into dislike of him or distrust of his actions.

Dealing with Offenses

Offense defined, according to Webster's New World Dictionary in English, means: 1. a sin or crime 2. a creating of resentment, displeasure 3. a feeling hurt, angry, etc. 4. something that causes anger, etc. 5. the act of attacking 6. the side that is attacking or seeking to score in a contest.

The Greek word for "offense" means a snare, a causing to sin. Therefore, an offense can be a sin, a crime against someone else, or the response to a sin or crime against one's self. From these definitions, we can see why we need the Law of Anger to regulate our response to offenses. Jesus told His disciples that it was impossible that occasions of stumbling or offenses should not come (Luke 17:1), but woe unto them through whom they come. James says (James 3:2) "He who offends not in word, the same is a perfect man." Thus, we have a responsibility not only to respond correctly, but also to refrain from causing offense to others.

He that cannot be offended is dead! Just imagine someone standing over a casket hurling insults at a corpse. What a ridiculous pose! A dead man can be insulted all day long and never respond. We hail this as the ideal condition of the fleshly mode, but, alas, it cannot be implemented in an instance. It must be put into practice by learning, often through many failures. When an irritated attitude is firmly established, the next step is to verbalize feelings. In exasperation, we call the offending one a derogatory name: "Raca!" (Worthless one), in our family it was "Dumkauf!" ("Dumb head" in German.) Perhaps in your family it was: "Stupid!"

Now we have involved our brother in our anger, and will certainly evoke a response from him in defense of himself. Conflict between two individuals becomes the breeding ground of bitterness. If we continue to feed our attitude of dislike or even dismissal, we categorize the other individual, putting him into a psychological box that he can sense from our body language. He then becomes bitter at us. But, in frustration, under our condemnation, he probably will do even worse.

That can bring us to the stage of complete character assassination: "You Fool!" In the conflict Jesus deals only with the initiator of anger. Later in Matthew, repeating His words in Luke 17:1, Jesus told His disciples, "It must needs be that offenses come, but woe unto that man by whom they come (Matthew 18:7). Consequently, the law of anger deals with the offender first.

> **If therefore thou art offering thy gift at the altar, and there rememberest that thy brother hath aught against thee, leave there thy gift before the altar, and go thy way, first be reconciled to thy brother, and then come and offer thy gift. Agree with thine adversary quickly,** *while thou art with him in the way;* **lest haply the adversary deliver thee to the judge, and the judge deliver thee to the officer, and thou be cast into prison. Verily I say unto thee, thou shalt by no means come out thence, till thou have paid the last farthing.**
>
> **Matthew 5:23-26 AV (Emphasis added)**

Undoubtedly, the Holy Spirit prompts one to remember offending someone when he brings a peace offering to be sacrificed at the temple altar. Because God places the responsibility of attempting restoration squarely on the offender, He requires reconciliation before the offender's gift can be received. In this case, it was probably the offender's anger that caused the offense in the first place. If each person dealt with his own anger, before it affected someone else, we would live in a peaceful world.

Suppose you are the offender. What should you do? Jesus' solution to the problem was: recognize your anger as a potential to sin. Don't try to gloss over it by worshipping, giving, or any other religious act. Instead, deal with the problem with the person directly asking for forgiveness without blaming him for your anger. Perhaps there is reason for his action that irritates, one that you cannot see. Investigate, and then try to understand.

Perhaps he can be helped to overcome the fault. In any case, you need to come to an agreement with him while a relationship still exists (whiles thou art in the way with him). If you don't, the relationship may deteriorate to the point that he may report your offense to others.

Jesus said that he that is angry without cause is in danger of the judgment. Even if the anger has not progressed to the name calling stage, your attitude will be seen in the spirit of the one offended. (Remember the spirit displays our emotions in body language.) Others may even pick up your attitude and make value judgments against you.

At this point the judgment is just against an attitude. But if you insult your brother further by calling him a name or worse, you slander him by expressing his fault to others. Now you are in danger of the condemnation of other brethren (the council) because the offense is now public and you have attacked your brother. Or the slander could draw others to your side of the conflict causing a division among brethren. This is one of the things God hates (Proverbs 6:19).

The council referred to in Jesus' day would have been the Sanhedron, but in the New Testament era would refer to the Church. Now that the offense is public, the offended has recourse against you to present it publicly, for Jesus also said concerning the offended one:

> **And if thy brother sin against thee, go, show him his fault between thee and him alone: if he hear thee, thou hast gained thy brother. But if he hear thee not, take with thee one or two more, that at the mouth of two witnesses or three every word may be established. And if he refuse to hear them, tell it unto the whole assembly (or church): and if he refuse to hear the church also, let him be unto thee as the Gentile and the publican.**
>
> **Matthew 18:15-17 AV**

If the one you offended follows these instructions, he will not develop a bitter response to the offense of name-calling or slander, but will rather examine himself to see if a basis for the irritation exists. However, the fault of both you and he will be exposed if he takes it to the assembly of the whole church. If he can admit his weakness and try to do better, this may restore the relationship. But then, you would have to admit your lack of patience (longsuffering) and confess your anger. If you insist on branding him, or further insult him by calling him a fool, you end up revealing to everyone your own lack of character. If the verdict of the Church is refused by either of you, and an unforgiving spirit persists, a spiritual prison of bitterness results. Demonic spirits overrun an unforgiving spirit and bring him into bondage. They do this by continually focusing the man on his resentments, causing the bitterness to flavor his whole life.

How much better it is to show mercy by controlling your anger, forgiving the other's fault, and suffering his weakness.

Law of Anger Diagrammed

Irritation--------------------Attitude vented by body language
Exasperation---Name Calling
Dismissal as a Fool---------------------Character Assassination

Although we have already looked at the law in general, we need to recognize the three stages of anger, knowing one will progress to another if not stopped. Then we need to stop it at the first stage. Controlling your spirit develops the fruit of meekness. Let us look at these three stages so that you can recognize them when they appear.

Developing Meekness—First Stage Anger: Without Cause

The word translated "without cause" in the original means idly, through the idea of failure (weakness). The weakness may be of the body, or some failure of the mind or a character fault. The following are some examples.

Making a mess by being incompetent—a small child spills a glass of milk. We get angry at the waste or the mess. An older child is careless or awkward; as a result he knocks something off and breaks it. Anger comes from the loss of the broken object.

An elderly person acts childish, causing the daughter or son to act like a parent over him. Anger comes from impatience at the decrepitude of old age, the young having not experienced mental breakdown that comes with age.

A driver makes a mistake in traffic. Anger stems from slowing us down or endangering us.

A friend fails to return something borrowed, showing irresponsibility, costing you money or time.

These irritations arise from an inconvenience to you. All of these were the result of weakness or failure. Your child did not intend to spill the milk, but he has not yet gained complete control over his hands. Your older child did not intend to break the object; he was simply being careless. Your elderly father or mother does not intend to frustrate you, but his or her mind no longer thinks clearly. The driver may not intend to cause you a traffic problem; he just made a wrong decision or was being selfish. That's his fault, but what can you change by being angry? Your borrowing friend, having met his own need, has failed to think of yours. All these things cause irritation to rise in people nearby.

In God's eyes, we are condemning because of weakness—anger without cause. He remembers that we are but dust, full of frailty and incompetence. We need to remember that, too. If we recognize our weaknesses, we can forgive another's weakness. It can become a signal to help people overcome a fault and improve themselves. Recognizing weakness diffuses the irritation before it becomes an attitude of disapproval.

Broadcast disapproval can affect a crowd. Euodia and Syntuche were disrupting the peace of the church in Philippi so much that Paul had to write and urge them to be of the same mind. We are not told what the problem was, but if it had anything to do with their names, we suspect the problem.

The essence of the name "Euodia" means—"fine traveling, to help on the road, success in business affairs" In other places the same word is translated "prosperous." We can deduce that she was an organized and efficient lady who prospered in all her works.

"Sntyche," on the other hand, means—"an accident," which comes from another word which means "to chance together." If the name describes the lady, then she is just the opposite of Euodia. Syntyche probably was totally unorganized and haphazard in her affairs. This flaw was probably a weakness that irritated Euodia greatly and provoked her to offend Syntyche with an angry criticism—anger without cause in God's eyes.

The usual result of irritation is angry words. And what is worse, we vent our anger toward the person rather than the action. Euodia probably vented her irritation, otherwise Paul would never have heard about it. Syntyche was offended. She probably retorted with angry words. Paul admonished them both to be of the same mind.

If Euodia had kept the irritation to herself, Syntyche would not have been offended. On the other hand, if Syntyche had not responded in anger but promised to do better, the dispute might have dissolved. James gives good advice on this account.

> **But let every man be swift to hear, slow to speak, slow to wrath: for the wrath of man worketh not the righteousness of God.**
>
> **James 1:19, 20 AV**

Being slow to speak gives opportunity to determine the reason for the source of irritation. It also gives time to diffuse the anger. Words can then be directed toward the deed and how to overcome this fault in the future. A soft voice and gentle spirit may help enlist the cooperation of the weak one.

Lowering our expectations of others also helps lower irritation. If we expect a certain standard, and he or she does not reach it, we often explode. Again, this is a signal that they need help.

Learning to forgive the weakness quickly seems to lessen our irritations over all. It is a divine response after much practice. Flying into a rage shows the natural response, also much practiced. Stopping the irritation at the start, shows that the Holy Spirit is steadily producing control over our emotions. Meekness is control. The Spirit alone has the power to eliminate life's irritations and produce this meekness.

Second Stage Anger: with Cause

In his seminars, teacher Bill Gothard deals at length with anger. He says that most anger stems from injured individual rights. We live in a day when everyone seems to demand his rights. We have women's rights, racial rights, and gay rights, etc. Gothard has isolated and listed certain inalienable rights that we all feel we have. Briefly listed they are:

1. My right to express my opinion without angry retorts.
2. My right to be accepted.
3. My right to plan my time.
4. My right to have privacy.
5. My right to earn and spend money.
6. My right to choose friends.
7. My right to control the use of my belongings.

Interfere with any of these "so called" rights and you provoke a dispute. Let's look at how this may happen,

For example, take the voiced opinion. A man's opinion expresses what is in his heart. If you ridicule or flatly contradict it, you have ridiculed or contradicted the man himself. Thus, the man feels threatened and gives an emotional response, usually anger.

Now take the second presumed right. A business refuses to hire a qualified man because of his ethnic background. He is incensed at being rejected upon his nationality alone. He has a right, doesn't he?

Or maybe it's the right to be accepted as he sees himself. If you put down what he thinks he is, he will either be hurt, causing an offense, or angry, and lash back.

If you think about it, all find all these rights, when interfered with, provoke anger. An honest and upright person will do what he can to avoid stepping on the rights of others.

But what if they step on yours? Now your anger has a cause. Will you respond to your natural inclination and scream, "You idiot!" Or worse, depending upon how accomplished you are at telling people off, or will you let it seethe deep down in your emotions, collecting, and smoldering until the day you explode at a "last straw?"

Meekness does not require that you let the offense go without response. It simply keeps you under control when you do respond. The anger is real and deserved, but it must not be out of control. Therefore, the correct way to handle the situation is to confront the person "while you are in the way;" while the incident is still fresh. Confront him with the deed, calmly as possible, but do not attack his personality. If he points out wrong on your part, admit it and ask forgiveness. This should dissolve small disputes, because if you admit your fault he will probably admit his, so you can forgive him.

If he will not hear you, you have recourse to the Matthew 18 instruction by taking witnesses to establish the truth. If that doesn't clear it up, then take it to the whole church.

Suppose the person giving offense is not a Christian, then what? Treat it the same as any offense. If the act is Civil or Criminal, you can resort to the courts. One caution, however, the Word forbids you to go to court against your brother in the Lord. Paul says it is better to take the wrong and be defrauded, than to prosecute (1 Corinthians. 6:1-8). This way God becomes his judge.

If the offender is a friend, confront him gently with his fault that offends. If he hears, forgive him. If not, forgive him anyway for you own relief from bitterness. Lower your expectations of him, and take measures to protect yourself from his fault. For instance, suppose his fault is carelessness, then you don't lend him your fine machinery. Another solution according to Bill Gothard, is to lay down your rights to your possessions by giving them to God. If you do this, you make God responsible to take care of the offense. All you do is forgive. If you give God your possessions and someone damages them, then God becomes your claims agent. He will restore it if he chooses and attend to the retribution of the offender. Remember, it is his to do with as he pleases because you gave it to him.

Gothard, having given his car to God was rear-ended in an accident. He reminded God that it was His car. But he, Bill, no longer had transportation. Since it was God's car, he replaced it. In fact, Bill Gothard was given seven cars to replace it. I am sure God gave him this special illustration because of his teaching, but you have to admit it is an example that illustrates the principle very well.

In conclusion, anger with cause can be diffused by gentle controlled confrontation or by laying down your rights. In either case you forgive the other person and trust God to be your avenger if need be. Forgiveness is necessary to prevent bitterness from forming in your own heart.

Third Stage Anger: Complete Character Assassination

This stage of anger cannot be reached without passing through at least one of the other two stages. Irritation continually indulged will lead to name-calling, and if not checked ends in complete character assassination. An angry burst of "You fool!" becomes the final blow to one's ego. No one, absolutely no one, wants to be thought of as a fool, much less called one.

Calling someone a fool may end the relationship, sometimes violently. Perhaps this is the reason the Scripture maintains that he who calls another a fool is in danger of hellfire. The response to his anger has been set on fire of hell by demons in his opponent, as James suggests of the tongue (James 3:6). Once demons are involved, the anger becomes amplified in both parties.

Anger opens a door in the spiritual world for demons to enter the situation because of the strife (James 3:15, 16). For example, in a dispute, anger builds up between the parties. As it grows hotter and hotter, one strikes out at the other just to harm, but instead he kills his opponent.

He did not intend to kill, but the excess anger generated access to his spirit by demons. They added extra energy to his spirit when he struck, along with a momentary desire to kill. We call this a hot-blooded killing. Calling someone a fool may just be the final fuel to provoke such an act.

Anger of the smoldering kind may not kill right away but builds up secretly in the heart. Yet, Hell-fire generates it the same as the hot-blooded anger. This is known as malice. Alfred P. Gibbs, an old Brethren preacher friend of mine, defined malice as "anger, boiled down and served cold." It festers, seethes, and finally decides that the worthless one, thought of as a fool, no longer deserves to live or perhaps he seeks revenge for the offense caused. In either case, he plans the murder and carries it out in cold blood. On the other hand, perhaps it is the offended one who harbors the malice and strikes back.

In both instances, the anger has extra fire-power added because spirits get involved. A scriptural example is King Saul of the Old Testament. Saul's anger against David began with jealousy. This was anger without cause because David did not provoke it. It progressed straight to the third stage anger because of a spirit. (1 Sam. 18:10). At this point Saul hurled a javelin, intending to impale David to the wall. David simply avoided it and Saul. Next, Saul schemed against David by marrying him to his spirited daughter, Michal. When this didn't work because of Michal's affection for David, he threw the javelin again. Missed again. David fled for his life, and Saul, now fully charged with hell-fire and malice, pursued. He was fully committed to the third stage of anger.

By avoiding Saul, David kept himself free from anger. He laid down his rights and trusted God. In the end, God judged Saul and punished him. David was free of guilt.

In another incident, David proved his restraint of anger. When his son Absalom took over his kingdom, as David was leaving Jerusalem, Shimei called him a son of Belial and cursed him. Instead of striking back, he accepted the abuse.

It was not forgotten, however. Years later, when David turned his kingdom over to Solomon, he asked him to render justice (1 Kings 2:8, 9). Solomon confined Shimei to the city limits of Jerusalem. If he left the city, the death sentence would be imposed, thus his fate was in his own hands. He left, bringing death upon himself. Thus, justice was rendered leaving both David and Solomon free of blood-guiltiness.

Anger of the third degree fills one with bitterness, especially if he refuses to forgive the offense. Jesus gave a classic example of the bondage imposed upon a bitter, unforgiving person in His parable of the unforgiving servant.

The servant of the parable owed the king ten thousand talents. (We are not told if this is gold or silver.) If it was in gold, (according to values at the time of this writing), he owed the king $290,850,000. If it was silver he only owed the king $19,400,000. The king forgave his debt. The servant's fellow servant owed him $1.00, which he refused to forgive. When the king found out, he had the unforgiving servant delivered to tormentors until he paid all he owed.

The explanation of the parable is this: We are the servants, God is the king, and the tormentors of the bitterness prison are demons. If we don't forgive our brethren, God will not forgive us. Bitterness locks the door to God's grace and opens it to demons. Unchecked anger leads to bitterness, which always leads to bondage.

But if that is not bad enough, bitterness also reproduces itself. The writer of Hebrews tells us that we should look diligently, "lest any man fail of the grace of God; lest any root of bitterness springing up trouble you, and thereby *many be defiled*" (Hebrews 12:15). The tree of bitterness sprays seeds of anger on all those around it. These seeds lodge in other lives, causing more trees to take root. No wonder Gothard calls bitterness a main root of other problems.

The Marks of a Meek Man

Meekness goes hand in hand with several of the other fruits. For instance, a meek man is also a patient man, willing to suffer the shortcomings of others. A meek man is a humble man, not easily irritated by slights to his character. A meek man is a man of faith who trusts God with his possessions or time and is not constantly bickering over his so-called rights. A meek man is a loving man, giving away unselfishly to the needs of others. Meekness, then, means controlling our emotions and producing an even-tempered personality. This does not mean that meek men are never angry. Anger is a legitimate emotion. The Scripture says that God is angry at the wicked everyday (Ps. 7:11). If a Holy God can be angry and be righteous, then so can men. God is the supreme example of how to manage anger.

Though he is angry at the wicked every day, the Scriptures give example after example of his compassion and long-suffering before he executes wrath upon them. Take Israel, for example. He sent prophets to warn generations before he actually poured out his wrath. Righteousness demands that justice be rendered. Wickedness always injures someone. Therefore, to not be angry at injustice is to condone it. Thus, a meek man is angry at the wickedness and injustice, just like God. If he is truly meek, he controls his anger and channels it to bring about justice.

Designed to preserve our relationships with others, the law of anger presents three stages of anger. The first, irritation at weaknesses, God declares is without cause, therefore, unwarranted. The second degenerates into name calling, which provokes a response. The third totally demeans and destroys the character of the object of anger, heating up the dispute to a dangerous level. The law also offers the solution to relationship problems: agreement or forgiveness. The end-result in obeying this law is meekness.

6

Treasure Versus Pleasure: The Law of Purity

Adultery is the worst-case scenario to the purity law because it is not just a crime against God, but also against one's marriage partner and the breaking of a vow. Again, Jesus starts His law at the heart level. He says:

> **Ye have heard that it was said, Thou shalt not commit adultery:** *but I say unto you,* **that every one that looketh on a woman to lust after her hath committed adultery with her already in his heart.**
>
> **Matthew 5:27, 28AV (Emphasis added)**

God shows Himself to the pure in heart, as the beatitude says, because God loves purity. Jesus said, "none is good, save one, that is God." Purity is the highest form of goodness as it includes chastity. The Law of Purity develops goodness. Since it is God's own nature, to be pure in heart is to be like God. Being like-minded attracts God to a relationship with us.

All the gods worshipped by the nations were just the opposite. They were licentious and immoral, as their myths portray. Even the worship rituals were an excuse to commit immoral acts since the priests and priestesses engaged in harlotry and perversion.

God does not condone nor participate (as some gays claim), rather He condemns their acts as "vile affections" and their minds as "reprobate" (Romans 1:26, 28). As Habakkuk 1:13 says, "Thou art of purer eyes than to behold evil, and canst not look upon iniquity . . ."

Sex is Pure in Marriage

Contrary to the sexual misconduct of the gods of the nations, God ordained marriage as a symbol of the relationship between himself and his people. Thus, marriage between two people of opposite sex is a picture of the union of God with his redeemed. That is why it is called Holy Matrimony. The writer of Hebrews states, "Marriage is honorable in all, and the bed undefiled: but whore mongers and adulterers God will judge" (Heb. 13:4). Therefore, any sex carried on outside of marriage is an immoral act in God's eyes.

If a higher standard of righteousness is to be obtained, than it will have to start with the heart, because according to Jesus, the heart is the source of evil. He says it again in Mark 7:21: "For from within, out of the heart of men, proceed evil thoughts, adulteries, fornications . . . ." But you say, that is all very well for the unsaved. What about Christians? Do they commit such things? Why must there be a law for the righteous?

Answer: because of the nature of the flesh. Galatians 5:19 states the works of the flesh as follows: Adultery, fornication, uncleanness, lasciviousness, plus a whole list unrelated to our subject. Paul told the Galatians that he had told them twice before, Those who do such things shall not inherit in the kingdom of God. If Christians live in the mode of the flesh, they can commit these acts (1 Corinthians. 5:1). Paul even accused some of the Corinthians as not having repented of the uncleanness, fornication and lasciviousness they had committed (2 Corinthians. 12:21). So, yes, we do need a law governing purity for Christians.

The "end time" Church is especially guilty of breaking this law. According to Jude, evil men creeping into the Church will turn the gospel into lasciviousness. It was also so in the last days of the prophets. Malachi lists adulterers with the sins to be judged in his day (3:5). He also states that the righteous spoke often to each other and thought upon the name of the Lord. These, God said, shall be my peculiar treasure and they shall return and judge the wicked.

Judging the wicked is the same as inheriting in the kingdom of God. That is why we titled this law Treasure versus Pleasure. It is better to be named as his peculiar treasure than to have a temporary pleasure in the flesh.

> **And if thy right eye causeth thee to stumble, pluck it out, and cast it from thee: for it is profitable for thee that one of thy members should perish, and not thy whole body be cast into hell.**
>
> **And if thy right hand causeth thee to stumble, cut it off, and cast it from thee: for it is profitable for thee that one of thy members should perish, and not thy whole body go into hell.**
>
> **Matthew 5:28-30 AV**

The Law of Purity limits the eye and the hand. It is only natural because lust enters the heart by the eye, and the hand motivated by such lust reaches out to take what is desired. By controlling the eye and the hand, we control lust. Plucking out the eye or cutting off the hand call for severe measures, but not a solution, because they would not prevent our seeing or getting with the other eye or hand. So what is the Lord talking about?

Lust fires the emotions like nothing else. To keep it under control requires drastic measures. Lust, once entertained, moves on into the spiritual realm. Job declares that he made a covenant with his eyes: "Why then should I think upon a maid?" (31:1). Remember, Jesus said, whoever lusted after a woman had already committed adultery with in his heart. That means his mind had fantasized the event, calling upon his spirit's creative imagination.

James 1:14 says that man is tempted when he is drawn away by his own lust and enticed, then when sin is conceived (the creative imagination works on it until he commits the act), sin is born. The act of adultery gives birth to the sin, but impurity begins long before they reach the bed. Just as the Law of Anger puts the responsibility solely upon the offender, the Law of Purity puts the responsibility upon the man. Perhaps this is because, physically speaking, the man must cooperate or there is no sexual act. A woman, being weaker in physical strength, cannot force a man. Joseph fled leaving Potiphar's wife standing, holding his garments. Neither her desires nor her wiles could force him to participate.

Man's Part

I can almost hear you men complaining—"It's not fair, It's only natural for us to respond to what we see. It helps with the mating process." That is entirely true. But after you have chosen a mate, strict controls must be placed upon this natural trait. Your longing eyes must be for your wife alone. As Job reported, he made a covenant with his eyes not to lust after what he saw. This covenant existed between his eyes and his mind. He would not think upon a maid.

Herein lies the secret to stopping lust. Do not allow the mind to entertain impure thoughts. This does not mean you have to cover your eyes when an attractive woman walks by. Two men of God were walking on the beach when two shapely young girls walked by them in bikinis. The older man turned to the younger and said, "Oh, didn't God do a good job, when he made them?" He was able to appreciate their beauty without it creating lust. He had learned to be at peace with his own heart.

This will not work, however, if through continual indulgence of lusting, a man has been brought into spiritual bondage. Remember, spirits can read our body language. They are on the lookout for foolish young men, filled with sexual virility. Lust spirits hang around the magazine department where girlie magazines are sold, ready to pounce upon those who would indulge their eyes. I know of a woman who experienced their power herself, when she accidentally came across some old, coverless magazines hidden in her son's room. She opened the pages to see if the magazines were useful, or just some trash, not even suspecting the nature of them. The picture of a naked woman, in a very provocative position, attacked her eyes. She quickly shut the magazine, stinging with anger that it should even be in her son's room, much less in *her* house. She said, "All day long the picture was forced upon my mind. It was a struggle to keep it out. If that picture could attack my mind so powerfully, me, who did not want to look at it, what would it do to a willing subject?"

I have heard that today many men have become addicted to pornography, even pastors, because it is so easily available on the internet. If you are such a one, there is hope of freedom. Maybe you have already recognized the fact that thoughts of lust can be forced upon you against your will. Once a spirit gets involved in your life, you can lose the struggle to control the mind, that's how powerful these types of spirits can be. When a spirit gets an open channel to your spirit, he sends powerful suggestions that can override your own thinking. He has a right to do this because of the sin of lusting.

Don't think just looking is a harmless activity hurting no one else. Much of the sexual abuse today can be laid at the feet of pornography. Demons drive the urgency to go beyond (entice James 1:14) and indulge in sexual activity. Many a Pastor has fallen as a result. But that is not the worst that can happen. Paul warns Christians of the power of such sins.

> **Now the works of the flesh are evident, which are: adultery, fornication, uncleanness, lewdness, idolatry, sorcery, hatred, contentions, jealousies, outbursts of wrath, selfish ambitions, dissensions, heresies, envy, murders, drunkenness, revelries, and the like; of which I tell you beforehand, just as I also told you in time past, that those who practice such things will not inherit the kingdom of God.**
>
> **Galatians 5:19-21 AV**

All the sins above can disqualify you from inheriting the coming kingdom of God. He warned the Corinthian Church of the same thing (1 Corinthians 6:9, 10).

The first step in getting rid of a demon is to stop enjoying the sin. Repent and confess your sin, and ask God's forgiveness, thereby putting it under the blood, which cancels the demon's right to your life. Then call upon the authority of the name of Jesus—speak to the Demon of lust saying: "In Jesus' name, Sexual Lust, I command you to leave my body!" and mean it. He can tell by your attitude whether you really mean it! However, it is a dangerous thing to do if you don't intend to pursue righteousness, because the demon can return and bring seven more with him of even worse demons creating greater bondage (Matthew 12:43-45; Luke 11:24-26).

It is your right as a Christian to cleanse your spirit, because you sit *in Christ in heavenly places, which is above all powers and principalities* (Ephesians 2:5,6; 1:20-23) . Command the demon of Sexual Lust.(addressing him by his name) to come out! He probably has a companion named Fantasy Lust. You might need to command him to leave, too. They have no choice but to obey. If this is a sin done in secret, it can be confessed to God in secret and the demons dispatched, also in secret, saving public exposure. Who knows after you have been set free, perhaps you may help others so tormented. Freed from bondage,[4] it is only a matter of putting the flesh to death. Naked women could parade before a dead man all day long and he wouldn't even turn his head.

But if men insist on feeding their minds (in the flesh) with porn, girlie magazines, or X-rated material, spiritual bondage will grow stronger and stronger. The sad part of

---

[4] I include this information on deliverance because many Christians are ignorant of the power of demons to enter livesof those consciously committing sin. I worked in a deliverance ministry a short time in the past and have seen God set many free from demonic bondage.

this is if they will not forsake this sin, they will not inherit the kingdom's blessings promised to believers. God is just. He does not reward the unworthy. They are saved, but dwell in a separate place from the righteous.

Woman's Part

Even though the law does not specifically address women, New Testament writers speak of the need of women to dress modestly. Since lust begins in the eyes, Paul admonished men to lift up holy hands in prayer, and "in like manner also," the women adorn themselves in modest apparel. If the dress of the women in church is distracting, how can men lift up holy hands? I remember my husband complaining about some of the young girls back in the 60's, when short dresses barely covered their bottoms. It was distracting in church—of all places! It is the same today in some churches. Men recognize women "on the make" by their clothes or lack of them. Women need to recognize that fashions dictated by the world will only get more daring as the age progresses. Men will assess their character by the body exposure they allow themselves and consider them as fair game for sexual overtures.

The strange woman of Proverbs 7 met her prey with the attire of a harlot, even though she was a religious woman, just come from paying her vows at the temple. She was also married. Bathsheba, left home alone by her soldier husband, stripped down to bathe in full view of David's roof. How else would David have known how beautiful she was? From that distance I doubt if he saw her face.

What makes a woman want to dress to attract men? Answer: The seeking of pleasure and excitement, to get ahead financially, to attract another besides her mate; in short, a lack of purity. It's natural for women to want to be attractive. The right colors and appropriate lines can enhance natural beauty and still be modest. But the most attractive thing about a woman should be her character adorned with good works. Without that, she is like a beautifully wrapped present with nothing inside the box. The virtuous woman of Proverbs 31 wore purple, and dressed her children in scarlet. Her husband and her children praised her for her virtue, because purity shown out of her life in her works.

A pure heart comes from living in the confines of God's limits for sexual activity. Unclean thoughts defile the heart even if a deed is not forthcoming. Paul gives an apt conclusion to the matter. He says:

> **For this is the will of God, even your sanctification, that ye abstain from fornication; that each one of you know how to possess himself of his own vessel in sanctification and honor, not in the passion of lust, even as the Gentiles who know not God; that no man transgress, and wrong his brother in the matter: because the Lord is an avenger in all these things, as also we forewarned you and testified.**
>
> **For God called us not for uncleanness, but in sanctification. Therefore he that rejecteth [the admonition], rejecteth not man, but God, who giveth his Holy Spirit unto you.**
>
> **1 Thessalonians 4:3-7 AV**

If we want to belong to God's peculiar treasure and reign in the Kingdom to come, we will keep our heart pure for Him, and another fruit will be developed in our lives:— Goodness.

Faithfulness versus Unfaithfulness: The Law of Fidelity

> It was said also, Whosoever shall put away his wife, let him give her a writing of divorcement: *but I say unto you*, that every one that putteth away his wife, saving for the cause of fornication, maketh her an adulteress: and whosoever shall marry her when she is put away committeth adultery.
>
> **Matthew 5:31-34 AV (Emphasis added)**

This law covers the righteousness in keeping your word. In introducing this law, Jesus cited two Old Testament laws: the law concerning divorce and the law concerning forswearing. These are alike in that both of them involve making vows. A vow, or swearing an oath, means insuring your word as to truth or making a promise of future action. Webster's New World Dictionary defines "vow" as: 1. a solemn promise, especially one made to God 2. a promise to love and fidelity (in marriage) to promise or declare solemnly.

Webster's Dictionary defines "taking an oath" as: 1. "a declaration based on an appeal to God that one will speak the truth, keep a promise, etc. 2. the profane use of name, as in anger 3. a swearword, curse. "He defines "forswear" as "to deny or renounce an oath, to commit perjury," therefore, making a vow, or taking an oath means we make promises of commitment to someone. To forswear means we break our word to that commitment. To forswear in a court of law means to bear false witness under oath, a serious crime in God's eyes.

We use word commitments in many areas of our life. Marriage is the first and most obvious. Civil and criminal courts use oaths for swearing in witnesses. Religious orders use vows to bond their subjects. Then too, we often make vows to God for certain periods of time. In all these, it becomes tantamount that we keep our word. But Jesus says that righteousness requires more than just keeping vows. Your word in any matter should be your bond; and there should be no need to assure it with an oath. Say what you will do then do what you say.

Being unfaithful to your word is a cousin to lying. Lying deals with unfaithfulness to the truth either in the past or the present but cannot reach into the future. Promises deal only with the future. To break them has the same effect upon the conscience as lying. Therefore, keeping your word brings peace to the conscience; breaking it, just the opposite.

Faithful words bring peace, but unfaithful words bring conflict. Whether they apply to a marriage relationship or a family matter, if you break your promises, the peace in the relationship is broken. Suppose you promised your child a trip to the amusement park on Saturday. He was really counting on that promise, but you changed your mind on a whim, or worse, you forgot. What do you think would happen to your relationship with him? Suppose you promised your wife a trip to Europe, but then you saw a sweet new car you'd rather have. Would this bring peace in your relationship?

Suppose the promise was in the form of treaty between nations. One nation agreed to come to the aid of another in case of aggression from a third. What would happen if the treaty nation joined the attacker? War! Peace loses anytime a word is broken. If you break your word, you lose peace of conscience. If someone else breaks his word to you, the relationship suffers a lack of peace. If nations break their word in treaties, diplomatic relations break down.

Therefore, a broken word disturbs the peace no matter to whom it is broken. Hosea, speaking of the sins of Israel, says, "They make many promises, take false oaths and make agreements; therefore lawsuits spring up like poisonous weeds in a plowed field" (Hosea 10:4 NIV). No doubt, this is particularly true in business. On the other hand, keeping your word keeps the peace.

The peace of God stems from the fact that He always keeps his word. His promises are sure, whether they promise us blessing for keeping his word or cursing for breaking it. He will do what he says he will do. He wears the title of the God of Peace, because in the end he has the last word. As sovereign God he is the ultimate peace officer.

The fidelity law is broken into two parts: divorce and forswearing. First, let's look at divorce.

Divorce

The marriage vow states "as long as ye both shall live." Divorce breaks that vow. In this higher form of righteousness, Jesus says the only exception can be an act of harlotry, including adultery or incest.

Paul confirms this law when he says, "And unto the married I command, yet not I, but the Lord, Let not the wife depart from her husband: But and if she depart, let her remain unmarried, or be reconciled to her husband: and let not the husband put away his wife" (1 Corinthians. 7:10, 11).

Again, let me emphasize we are talking about higher righteousness. Adultery had a different solution under the Ten Commandments. According to the Old Testament law, adulterers were put to death, leaving the innocent one free to marry again. Since we do not put adulterers to death today, the only way to attain this higher righteousness is to remain unmarried when your spouse transgresses, at least until the transgressor remarries and all hope of reconciliation is past.

The consequences of breaking this law places blames securely the one causing the divorce. It forces his mate to remain unmarried or to marry someone else. In this case, the Lord charges him with multiple counts of adultery, his own, his new wife (and her former husband if she was married before), his former wife and her new husband. It could be an almost endless chain of adultery depending upon how many people are involved. This is quite a heavy load of sin to answer to before the Lord at the judgment seat of Christ, where he measures righteousness.

Yes, adultery can be forgiven. Jesus Himself forgave the woman taken in adultery. But we are talking about the higher righteousness now possible because we have the Spirit of God. If we would attain this righteousness, we will work out our problems with our spouse. It all comes down to the will. Will we obey and serve God or will we serve our flesh?

Foreswearing

All oaths or vows are sworn before God. That means He has the right to prosecute if they are not performed. To avoid foreswearing Jesus says don't swear at all. He further says why:

> **Again, ye have heard that it was said to them of old time, Thou shalt not forswear thyself, but shalt perform unto the Lord thine oaths:** *but I say unto you,* **swear not at all; neither by the heaven, for it is the throne of God; nor by the earth, for it is the footstool of his feet; nor by Jerusalem, for it is the city of the great King.**
>
> **Neither shalt thou swear by thy head, for thou canst not make one hair white or black. But let your speech be, Yea, yea; Nay, nay: and whatsoever is more than these is of the evil one.**
>
> **Matthew 5:34-37 AV (Emphasis added)**

Don't use heaven to swear by; it is God's, not yours. Furthermore, it is his throne, the place from which all authority stems. Don't use earth to swear by, either. It, too, belongs to God and all the authority from the throne rules over it. Don't swear by Jerusalem, because it is the seat of the great King Jesus when he comes into his power. Don't swear by your own head. Even that is under his control. In other words, you have no right to swear by anything that is God's.

In truth, none of these will help you keep your word, if you choose not to keep it. By swearing oaths, you attempt to convince someone else that you will keep your word. The more sureties you use, the weaker your word becomes. When you have to constantly swear, it means your word is not good by itself. That's why Jesus says, "Say yes when you mean yes and no when you mean no"; and then stick by it, no matter what. Anything more may just be to cover a deception, where you say you will do such and such, although you have no intention to do so. A false promise, as I said before, is a cousin to a lie.

A negative form of swearing takes the Lord's name in vain. A declaration such as "God damn you," is a curse. Since you clearly do not have the authority to do this, you are in effect assuming authority and usurping God's. Such expressions do not obligate God, but do give a word and a will for the enemy to work upon. Such words carry the same weight in the evil spiritual kingdom as prayer does in God's kingdom. Curses can often continue down through generations. We would all do well to free ourselves from curses dealt to our ancestors by breaking them in the name of Jesus, who broke the power of the curse by his death (Galatians 3:13).

In conclusion, faithfulness to your word brings the positive effect of peace, an extremely important fruit. Peace of conscience rests within, and peace of circumstances pervades your relationship with others. Keeping the peace means staying within God's word, and under his authority, letting his peace rule in your heart (Colossians 3:15). Exhorting others to keep their word makes you a peacemaker.

It is the proper attitude to have toward His authority. God never breaks his word. He remains ever faithful. His peace breaks over us when we do the same. Blessed are the peacemakers.

Retaliation versus Consideration:
The Law of Flexibility

The law of flexibility teaches us how to suffer even though we are in the right. The Old Testament Law insured justice demanding "an eye for an eye and a tooth for a tooth." But higher righteousness calls for suffering loss in order to develop the fruit of gentleness.

> Ye have heard that it was said, An eye for an eye, and a tooth for a tooth: *but I say unto you*, resist not him that is evil: but whosoever smiteth thee on thy right cheek, turn to him the other also. And if any man would go to law with thee, and take away thy coat, let him have thy cloak also. And whosoever shall compel thee to go one mile, go with him two. Give to him that asketh thee, and from him that would borrow of thee turn not thou away.
>
> **Matthew 5:38-42 AV (Emphasis added)**

A natural response to being wronged is to get even. The supernatural response is to suffer it. Jesus says, "Do not fight back when you are personally attacked by evil." To fight back does not give any testimony to the power and grace of God. Also, a practice of fighting back develops a violent nature, not a gentle one. Rather, when you are slapped on the cheek, turn the other cheek. This accomplishes two things. First, it shows your temper to be under control. And second, it shows your assailant that you deliberately choose to let him accost you. That causes him to be totally at fault. In that case, God becomes your champion in justice. Paul said, "Dearly beloved, avenge not yourselves, but rather give place unto wrath: for it is written, Vengeance is mine; I will repay, saith the Lord" (Romans 12:19).

Jesus gave four different circumstances where we can suffer at the hands of the world system even though we are in the right. Each of these depicts a different aspect of an individual's life.

The Religious Court

Being slapped on the cheek depicts a religious situation. You stand in the right as far as God and the truth are concerned, but zealots, who are deceived, and yet have a recognized ecclesiastic power, attack you. Nearly every mention of being slapped on the cheek in Scripture is such a situation. Sanhedron zealots struck Jesus upon the face when he was tried before them at the high priest's house (Luke 22:64). This was the fulfillment of Micah's prophecy: "They shall smite the judge of Israel with a rod upon the cheek" (Micah 5:1).

In 1Kings 22:24, Zedekiah smote Micaiah on the cheek for prophesying the word of the Lord in truth. Micaiah was standing in the presence of a group of false prophets countermanding their word. Paul was also struck on the face when he was brought before the Sanhedron in Jerusalem

(Acts 23:1 , 2). So we can conclude that when we have the word of the Lord and ecclesiastic leaders oppose us, we can only be an effective witness if we turn the other cheek.

Fighting against a religious position brings division, not unity, strife not peace. Paul advised Timothy: "The servant of the Lord must not strive; but be gentle unto all men, apt to teach, patient, in meekness instructing those that oppose themselves; if God peradventure will give them repentance to the acknowledging of the truth; . . . "(2 Timothy 2:24, 25). This shows the assailant that you deliberately choose to let him accost you. That makes him totally at fault. In that case, God becomes your champion in justice. As Paul said before, God does the avenging.

The Civil Court

The second situation points to a civil court dispute case.

> **And if any man would go to law with thee, and take away thy coat, let him have thy cloak also.**
>
> **Matthew 5:40 AV**

Suing a man for his coat denotes a failure to repay a debt. A poor man, having nothing else to secure his loan, has given his coat as a pledge. Evidently, he is unable to pay. Thus, the lender prosecutes to take away his coat.

The law in Deuteronomy 24:10 governs the use of a poor man's pledge. The coat was to be returned each night, so he could sleep in it. To take away a poor man's coat shows a desperately greedy lender. By giving away the cloak (usually an outer garment) means the borrower is left naked. (Clothed only in under-garments was considered naked in those days.) The lender becomes twice as evil in the sight of all. As a result of this action, he may feel guilty and forgive the debt. If not, then he will answer to God for his hard heart.

Is there ever a miscarriage of justice in civil courts today? Of course there is. The same action applies here as in the religious situation. Do not fight back. Instead give more than is asked for. This puts a heavy strain of guilt on the one who sued wrongfully or refused to have pity on the poor.

If the prosecutor trusts in God, he can forgive the debt. God will repay him (Prov. 19:17). But if he insists on his due, if you are the prosecuted one, you can give more than was necessary. This gives a response that releases any bitterness. You could have given only what was required, but you did more. You reflected the attitude of Christ toward those who wrongfully convicted you of a crime. You willingly suffer it. By giving the cloak also, you emphasized you willingness to suffer the penalty. You choose to forgive rather than to be bitter. This exercises gentleness. God becomes your champion and repays your loss by recognizing your righteousness.

How does this translate into our society? How would we give our cloak also? In principle, we would simply give more than is asked, thereby freeing ourselves of bitterness, and leaving the justice to God.

The Government

> And whosoever shall compel thee to go one mile, go with him two.
>
> Matthew 5:41 AV

The third situation refers to a governmental ruling. In Jesus' day, the Roman soldiers kept the peace among the citizens of Judea. Bible teachers say that Roman law allowed a soldier to conscript a native Judean to carry his gear for one mile—in Roman measurements 3,000 cubits or 1,700 feet. The Judeans, being the conquered people, could only comply or suffer the consequences. Being forced by the government to do menial servitude brought great resentment and bitterness to the proud citizens.

Jesus offered a new and better response. Let your attitude be one of a willing servant. Do not do only what is asked or just. Go beyond. Willingly give the service of another mile. By willingly going that second mile, you have defused your anger of the requirement and probably won over your adversary. Now, by your suffering, you have gained the attention and perhaps the ear of your superior in authority.

Many a Christian suffering persecution from an oppressive governmental magistrate has won him over to Christianity by his attitude in righteousness. Nothing can be accomplished when we fight back.

The Neighborhood

Give to him that asketh thee, and from him that would borrow of thee turn not thou away.

Matthew 5:42 AV

The fourth and final life situation is the domestic scene. This deals with our relationship to other citizens in our neighborhood. My neighbor knocks at my door and asks to borrow a loaf of bread. Never mind that she has done this repeatedly and failed to replace it.

Or maybe it is for money that he asks. The natural response here would be refusal. Why should you give to one who never repays his debts? The answer: because of his lack. He who lacks is in poverty. Proverbs 22:7 says that the borrower is the servant to the lender. But Proverbs 19:17 also says that he that gives to the poor lends unto God and God will repay him. So to develop the attitude of gentleness, you need to have compassion on the one in need. Do not resent his asking, even if laziness is the reason for his poverty.

Give, and suffer loss, showing compassion for his lack. God will put righteousness to your account and reward you in heaven, if not here and now. Each of these four situations shows an area of your life where you can suffer, even though you are entirely in the right. Jesus said, "Blessed are those who are persecuted for righteousness sake: for theirs is the kingdom of heaven" (Matthew 5:10). They suffer the wrong righteously, because they expect the kingdom of heaven to be their recourse. They are appealing to a higher court. Their action precipitates two effects in their lives. First, suffering, as opposed to fighting, cultivates the fruit of gentleness. And second, it brings reward in the kingdom, because those who suffer shall also reign, which we shall see later.

In turning the other cheek, they take note of the fact that religious leaders have been taken captive by the enemy and deceived. That frees them to be gentle in proclaiming the truth, which can have a more powerful effect on theologians than outright confrontation. In giving away their cloak, they recognize the injustice of the world, looking only to God for justice. Having suffered injustice, they know the pain of it firsthand. Submitting brings gentleness.

Submitting to the governmental authority establishes the proper attitude. God has commanded Christians to submit to the authorities over them. Even if the authority is corrupt, being a willing servant and going beyond the call of duty enlists their oppressor's admiration. Again, the result in the person is gentleness rather than a fighting spirit.

Giving to the poverty-stricken borrower develops compassion and unselfishness, which also contributes to gentleness. Therefore, gentleness becomes a full ripen fruit in the lives of those who respond correctly to suffering for righteousness sake.

The Usefulness of Suffering

Besides developing gentleness, an added benefit comes from obeying this law. Not only will their compensation come from the kingdom of heaven, but also their reward, because those that suffer will also reign. Paul told his son in the faith, Timothy, "If we suffer, we shall also reign with him:" . . . (2 Timothy 2:12).

He also told the Romans that "If we are children of God: And if children, then heirs, heirs of God, and jointheirs with Christ *if so be that we suffer with him that we may be also glorified with him*" (Romans 8:17). Peter also tells us that suffering brings the glorification.

> "But and if ye suffer for righteousness' sake, happy are ye: and be not afraid of their terror, neither be troubled [agitated].
>
> But sanctify the Lord God in your hearts and be ready always to give answer to every man that asks [the ecclesia, the court, the government, or the borrower] a reason of the hope that is in you with meekness and fear: . . . For Christ also hath once suffered for sins, the just for the unjust, . . . But rejoice, inasmuch as ye are partakers of Christ's sufferings; that when his glory

shall be revealed ye may be glad with exceeding great joy. . . . Yet if any man suffer for well doing, let him not be ashamed; but let him glorify God on this behalf"

(1 Peter 3:14, 15, 18, 4: 13, 16) AV

Again, Peter concludes: "The glory revealed as a result of suffering will reveal the joint-heirs of Christ, the Bride who shares His throne. Why will the sufferers reign? Because they know the sting and pain of injustice; they have been on the receiving end of miscarriage of justice. They, more so than others, can dispense fair judgment laced with compassion and mercy. They, as David, can declare: "Thy gentleness hath made me great" (Ps. 18:35). Therefore, the future kingdom will be furnished with administrators of justice, who have been fully trained by keeping this kingdom Law of Righteousness and who have developed this fruit: Gentleness.

9

Charity versus Hostility: The Law of Impartiality

The Law of Impartiality proposes to teach us charity by showing us how to love our enemies. If we can love enemies, we can love anyone, because this a true test of love.

> **Ye have heard that it was said, Thou shalt love thy neighbor, and hate thine enemy: but I say unto you, love your enemies, and pray for them that persecute you; that ye may be sons of your Father who is in heaven: for he maketh his sun to rise on the evil and the good, and sendeth rain on the just and the unjust.**
>
> **Matthew 5:43-45 AV**

Many words in the Scriptures are translated in to the English word "love." So to understand what Jesus meant by loving our enemies, we must first look at the actual Greek word he used.

Jesus said "agapao," which means more than just a feeling. Strong's says it involves the will as a matter of principle, duty and propriety. Contrast that with "phileo," which means friend or fond of, as to have an attachment to; a sentiment or feeling. Looking at the difference between the two, we see that Jesus is not asking us to treat our enemies as we would our friends, but to simply show them charity instead of hostility.

This statement means that we give them the same treatment God gives them, which is impartiality. He sends the rain on the just and the unjust. He extends mercy and grace to the sinner. Christ died for us when we were yet sinners and cut off from God. In short, we were God's enemies, and he extended grace.

God wants this character trait to develop in us so we will be like him, for God is love. Satan, on the other hand, acts just the opposite, because his character demands self-serving pride. He opposes God because he wants to take his place and he wants us to be just like him. He moves others against us and motivates their envy and competition. If we participate in the competition, we develop enemies and we emulate Satan's character. If we return evil for evil in retaliation, then we drop deeper into his attributes. This law exists for a reason, that we may not emulate the character of Satan but rather the character of God. Contrary to what most people think, hatred is not the opposite of love. That emotion goes with the former law concerning retaliation. The opposite of love is carelessness, foolishness and selfishness, especially selfishness.

The ultimate test of charity shows kindness and grace to an enemy. But is "agapao" love just as a duty as in the definition given earlier? Or does it encompass more? Paul's great chapter in I Corinthians 13 shows the full measure of "agapao" love. He says that without charity in our character we will be without reward or results from all our works, even though we go so far as to give our bodies to be burned. The reason? All works must be motivated from this characteristic of God to be worthy. Charity encompasses all of the other fruits of the Spirit. Listen to Paul's words. Notice the other fruits of the Spirit as well as the selflessness:

> **Charity suffers long, [long-suffering] and is kind [gentleness]; charity envieth not [self control]; charity vaunted not itself, is not puffed up [not proud like Satan], Doth not behave itself unseemly [purity] seeketh not her own [does not strive—peace], is not easily provoked [meekness], thinketh no evil [goodness]. Rejoiceth not in iniquity, but rejoiceth in the truth [joy], Beareth all things; believeth all things, hopeth all things, endureth all things [faith/faithfulness]. Charity never faileth . . .**
>
> 1 Corinthians 13:4-8aAV

Therefore, all the fruits are included in "agapao" love. No wonder then that John said, "God is love." A fine example of this would be a bunch of grapes. Each fruit of the Spirit, like each individual grape, is separate in and of itself and yet, they are all held together by one stem and each taste the same. In another metaphor, each fruit is one facet of a precious gem, each reflecting light from a different angle yet all belonging to the same stone. Charity is like that. God is like that.

The Adversary Exercises Our Agapao

Good character traits are best produced under adversity. God knows that to develop strength in anything, it must be exercised. For instance, if we would strengthen our muscles, we use counter weights for resistance. As we overcome the added weight, our muscles respond by developing greater strength and capacity. God does the same thing by allowing Satan to oppose the development of the fruits of the Spirit in us.

Only one place in the Old Testament speaks of hating enemies (Psalm 139:20, 21), and these are clearly those that rise up against God. "Do I not hate them, O Lord, that hate thee?" All other references to "hating" pertain to the sins committed by sinners. They are exhorted to hate the sin rather than the person. Old Testament believers were forbidden to hate their neighbors (Lev.19:17; Deut. 19:11). Therefore, we see from this the Old Testament standard only allowed you to hate those who hated God. Thus, the enemies we are talking about are enemies of God.

The more we stand for God and his righteousness, the more we become the target of the enemy, Satan. Consequently, when he becomes our enemy, he inspires all manner of people to rise up against us. This opportunity gives us opportunity to overcome and strengthen our character in the Lord, because the enemies of a righteous man are the enemies of God

On the other hand, if we fail to act in God's character, we will inevitably act in Satan's. To be hostile to those that oppose his way is natural to Satan. Taking sides and having a party spirit also demonstrates his way. By this method he has divided nations, churches, families and friends.

Agapao Glorifies God

Showing charity to enemies glorifies God, because it emulates his character. Many an enemy, acting under the influence of Satan, has been turned around by the graciousness of his victim. The sheer goodness of a man reveals itself to his human adversary and convicts him of his sin. Take the example of the jailer of Paul and Silas. When he would have killed himself, Paul said, "Do thyself no harm." Why should Paul have cared? Was not the jailer his enemy? No, Paul understood that men under authority act as they are bidden by the authorities. Paul did not have to preach to the jailer. He and Silas had sung and praised God in their cell. The jailer was aware of their activities. Paul's one act of concern, for his enemy's life, brought repentance to the jailer. That, plus the fact that they had not tried to escape, even though God had supernaturally provided a way, could have influenced him greatly.

Paul probably overheard the authorities charging the jailer to keep them safe. The jailer, in an attempt to comply with fear for his life, put them in the innermost chamber and then put their feet in stocks as well. Paul must have realized the peril of the jailer when God released them. His gracious good will showed itself to the jailer when he stopped him from committing suicide. As a result of his charity, he won the jailer and his whole family to Christ.

Enacting the Law

How do we show love? Let's look at how the law exhorts us to do that. Instead of hating (showing hostility), you are asked to do three things that show charity:

1. Bless those that curse you
2. Do good to those that hate you
3. Pray for those who despitefully use you or persecute you

Looking at each of these commands, we realize that they are completely opposite to natural inclinations. The natural response would be retaliation in like manner: a curse for a curse, evil for evil, and fighting back against attackers. Take the first command: Bless! What does it mean to bless? The dictionary says 1. to make holy, 2. ask divine favor for, 3. to make happy, 4. to praise.

Blessing is mostly a matter of using our lips. When we become agitated with an enemy, our natural inclination is to attack with words. Positive words bless; negative words tear down. Paul fulfilled this law when he blessed the jailer.

Curses bring demonic action and work like negative prayers. They give demons a will, and therefore a right, to work against someone. Imagine that you are walking through the Bazaar in Jerusalem's Moslem market. You stop to admire some merchandise in one of the booths. The Muslim proprietor endeavors to make a sale by hounding you with offers; but you walk on, ignoring his imploring words. Finally, assured he has lost a sale, he hurls the curses of Allah after you. Do you:

a. Walk off and ignore him.
b. Curse him back.
c. Bless him by asking divine favor for his soul.

Answer: c. You entreat the Lord to save him from his darkness. You might say something like this, "Lord Jesus Christ, bless this man and forgive his curses for he walks in darkness and does not know you." Is he your enemy? You bet he is, because he has been taught to hate Christianity by the spirit that drives Islam. In blessing him you recognize that it is a spirit, not the man, who curses you. Thus, you show impartiality as you see him as God sees him, lost and undone.

Now take the second command, Do good to them that hate you. This implies using your hands to accomplish some good deed. A distraught wife confessed her marital troubles to her pastor, whereupon he asked, "Have you tried heaping coals of fire upon his head?" referring to a passage in Romans 12. "No, Sir," she replied, "but I've tried boiling water." Paul says in Romans 12:20 "Therefore if thine enemy hunger, feed him; if he thirst, give him drink: for in so doing thou shalt heap coals of fire on his head."

Why should we do this? Because of the next verse, "Be not overcome of evil, but overcome evil with good." When we return good for evil, we may win over our enemy who sees our good and is convicted of his own bad behavior. God becomes our avenger, and we stay free of guilt, resulting in a clear conscience.

Finally the third command: Pray to release your enemy from the spirit that controls his mind. Prayer is a spiritual exercise that displays your attitude to God, one of impartiality, which is also God's attitude. Since you now agree, God is free to convict or judge according to your enemy's response. If you are being persecuted or despitefully used, it is because the spirit in charge of your oppressor hates God. Or, he is in service to an authority that hates God.

A good example of enemies winning their adversaries comes out of the Afghanistan war with Russia. Before the war the country was relatively devoid of Christianity. After the war many little Bible study groups were scattered across the nation. Christian Russian soldiers revealed Christ both in their lives and in the Word.

Another example is Jesus Himself at the cross. Actually, this is a good example of all three commands. When they began to pound the nails into his hands He said, "Father, forgive them, for they know not what they do." The soldiers pounding the nails were only obeying orders. Jesus had compassion on them. First, he blessed them. He asked divine favor for them. Then He did good for them by asking forgiveness for the act of crucifying God, a horrible crime.

He prayed for them that were despitefully using him. They were piercing his hands and his feet. Contrast his prayer and attitude with the thief that reviled and railed, even against Christ. The believing thief asked favor of Jesus and received it.

Jesus' prayer brought results. The centurion, after observing all that was said and how Jesus treated his enemies, glorified God, and said, "In very deed this man was just" (Luke 23:48). "Truly this [man] was the Son of God" (Matthew 27:54). I have no doubt that God later rewarded his faith with a full understanding of what Jesus accomplished that day. Perhaps we will meet this "enemy" in heaven.

How can we pray for our enemy? Pray for his spiritual eyes and ears to open, to see and hear the truth of the gospel. Pray for conviction of sin and for repentance. When we are able to do this, we show charity to our enemy. If we love only those who love us, where are we different from all the rest in the world? Jesus says even the publicans, the lowest of sinners, love their friends. The Laws of Righteousness demand a higher standard. God is impartial. He sends rain on the just and the unjust. Jesus concludes this law with the command: "Be ye therefore perfect, even as your Father which is in heaven, is perfect." When we obey this law, we learn how to suffer for Jesus' sake because the beatitude says: "Blessed are ye, when men shall revile you, and persecute you, and shall say all manner of evil against you falsely for my name's sake [because they are the enemies of God]. Rejoice and be exceeding glad: for great is your reward in heaven: for so persecuted they the prophets which were before you." Develop Love.

10

Sow Verses Show:
The Law of Devotion

This law concerns motives—devotion to God or devotion to self. The companion beatitude states: the kingdom of heaven belongs to the poor in spirit. Those who are poor, according to the Greek word "ptosso," are absolute beggars. They profess no strength in themselves and are, therefore, totally dependent upon God. God told Paul that when he was weak, then was he strong in the Lord. So, he reveled in his weakness. It is an extensive law covered in the following verses from Matthew 6:1 – 18.

> Take heed that you do not do your charitable deeds before men, to be seen by them. Otherwise you have no reward from your Father in heaven. Therefore, when you do a charitable deed, do not sound a trumpet before you as the hypocrites do in the synagogues and in the streets, that they may have glory from men. Assuredly, I say to you, they have their reward. But when you do a charitable deed, do not let your left hand know what your right hand is doing, that your charitable deed may be in secret; and your Father who sees in secret will Himself reward you openly.

"And when you pray, you shall not be like the hypocrites. For they love to pray standing in the synagogues and on the corners of the streets, that they may be seen by men. Assuredly, I say to you, they have their reward. But you, when you pray, go into your room, and when you have shut your door, pray to your Father who is in the secret place; and your Father who sees in secret will reward you openly. And when you pray, do not use vain repetitions as the heathen do. For they think that they will be heard for their many words.

"Therefore do not be like them. For your Father knows the things you have need of before you ask Him. In this manner, therefore, pray:

"Our Father in heaven, Hallowed be Your name.

Your kingdom come. Your will be done on earth as it is in heaven. Give us this day our daily bread.

And forgive us our debts, As we forgive our debtors.

And do not lead us into temptation, But deliver us from the evil one. For Yours is the kingdom and the power and the glory for forever. Amen.

"For if you forgive men their trespasses, your heavenly Father will also forgive you. But if you do not forgive men their trespasses, neither will your Father forgive your trespasses.

"Moreover, when you fast, do not be like the hypocrites, with a sad countenance. For they disfigure their faces that they may appear to men to be fasting. Assuredly, I say to you, they have their reward. But you, when you fast, anoint your head and wash your face, so that you do not appear to men to be fasting, but to your Father who is in the secret place; and your Father who sees in secret will reward you openly

Matthew 6:1-18 NKJV

The whole attitude here is humility, so that God may get the glory. Isaiah tells us that God dwells with a "contrite and humble spirit" (Isa. 57:15) as well as in the high and holy place. Remember the attitude of a man reveals itself in his spirit. Thus, a Christian who is poor in spirit can be rich in Godly motivation. On the other hand, developing the pride of life to become "somebody" curbs our effectiveness and usefulness to God. Doing religious acts for appearance sake puffs up the flesh. Gaining confidence from others shows a rich spirit, independent and self-reliant and without any need.

Fleshly pride also reflects the condition of Lucifer, the angel that fell because he reveled in the gifts and position God gave him. When he fell, he took a following with him, those who admired his ways. James 4:6 says that God resists the proud. Thus, Lucifer (the light bearer) became Satan (the adversary), and his angels followed him to become the enemies of God. We too, will imitate Satan if we promote ourselves by showing off.

Besides showing the proper attitude of a servant, this law also reveals the way to initiate work for the kingdom of heaven. It takes up three areas of Christian service that all servants may do: giving, praying, and fasting. However, faithful service attends to these tasks done in secret, so that God will get the glory.

In order to be effective at keeping the flesh out of our service, we need to understand what God has done. Hebrews 4:1 tells about God's rest that we are exhorted to enter. This rest refers back to creation. When God finished making the heavens and the earth, He rested on the seventh day. Whereupon Genesis 2:4 says, "These are the generations of the heavens and of the earth when they were created ("generations meaning descent, i.e. family, history). Genesis 2:1 states that the heavens and the earth were *finished* and all the host of them. The word finished here means completed. He accomplished all this by his Word. Further, Hebrews 1:3 tells us that he "upholds all things by the word of his power."

If the heavens and the earth were totally finished, if their host--every star, stone, animal or person that was to be, already made in his mind, that means God set things in motion on a pre-programmed schedule. Like a computer programmer, He wrote his Word into everything. As a result, everything done on the earth or in the stars follows one great plan. Any deviance from the plan may cause some turbulence but cannot scuttle it. Like a stone in the river standing against the current, it may cause ripples but the river flows on. The stone wears down by the action of the stream.

This is known in Scripture as God's will. He rests because the program is complete; all action continues on the program already put in force. I am not talking about individual predestination. We have some latitude of self-will within the confines of history. We make the choices, but God sets the consequences of those choices. That is his sovereign right!

What I am talking about is directing our lives to go with His flow. The only way we can enter into this rest is to cooperate with the program. If we go contrary to it, we are the ones who suffer, like the stones in the river. Rest, then, comes from finding out God's will in any matter of life and cooperating with it. In this way we become true servants accomplishing His work for His glory.

In resting in God's will we learn to trust God's Word, both the "logos" and the "rhema," the two Greek words for "word." When we see His glorious results, it fills us with faith (the fruit of this law) and makes us more faithful. But it must be done in secret to prevent the flesh from glorying before others or else we lose eternal rewards.

Giving

Take heed that you do not do your charitable deeds before men, to be seen by them. Otherwise you have no reward from your Father in heaven."

Matthew 6:1 AV

Webster's New World Dictionary states that Alms means taking pity upon the poor by giving money or food. The meaning in the Greek is compassionateness (toward the poor), a benefaction. Proverbs 19:17 says, "He that hath pity upon the poor lendeth unto the Lord: and that which he hath given will he pay him again." This, of course, is beyond tithing. We owe God a tenth of our income. Giving to the poor goes beyond this to alms.

Checking what God has to say about the poor in the Word, I find that very few books in the whole Bible fail to mention the poor. Jesus said, "The poor you always have with you, but me you have not always," in answer to the protest that the expensive ointment Mary used to anointed his feet should have been sold and money given to the poor. Deuteronomy 15:11 specifically states, "the poor shall never cease from the land." Paul exhorted the Ephesians to work with their own hands so they would have something to give to the needy (Ephesians 4:28). It seems, then, that the poor are specially designated by God as where to give alms in service to Him.

The Christians of the first church in Jerusalem sold their possessions in order to give to the poor brethren of their church. Thus, everyone had an adequate living. I think this is probably a good pattern. Rather than give to the poor indiscriminately, they made a testimony to the world of their love for the brethren.

Annaias and Sapphira spoiled this testimony when they kept back part of the money (Acts 5). They did it for show, because everyone else was doing it. But they really didn't want to give it all. The fault was not in keeping it back. As Peter said, it was their money to do with as they pleased. The sin was in letting others think they were giving it all. They were lying to the Holy Spirit in their brethren.

Cornelias was a devout Gentile who gave alms to the people and prayed to God. For this, God remembered him and sent Peter to preach the gospel to his household. Paul collected alms from the Gentile churches for his stricken countryman impoverished by drought.

God is compassionate and full of mercy. To give with that motive is to be like him. The purpose of these laws is to make us like our Father. To give to enhance our own reputation glorifies us. That robs God because all our substance comes from Him anyway.

Giving alms to ministries furthers God's kingdom. Jesus Himself lived from the contributions of others. He taught his disciples this principle when he sent them out two by two. Paul received funds from the Philippians and defended his right to receive them to the Corinthians, though he made his own living while among them. He told the Galatians, "Let him that is taught in the word communicate [give] unto him that teacheth in all good things" (Gal. 6:6). Let the teachers, pastors, etc. receive from their students.

This principle of "not muzzling the ox" supports the ministry that feeds "the sheep." This means that workers are entitled to eat from the harvest. If Christians didn't support full-time workers of the local church, who would? This was an established principle in the Old Testament and simply carried over into the Church. A tithe of one's assets went to support God's ministry at the temple.

The widow casting in her mite shows an example of the devotion to God found in giving. She gave all she had, trusting God to meet her future needs. Little did she know that Jesus took notice. Surely no man watching would think much of her gift, but Jesus was reading her heart.

Today, much of the Church charges the world to support its programs. Fund-raising becomes big business. As a result, the world sees little difference between itself and the Church.

But that is not God's way. He blesses individuals who are industrious and allows them to give in devotion to Him. When God is in charge of a project, the money flows in. When man is in charge, it comes slowly or dries up. Often this indicates God's will in a matter. If we give in to the world's methods in the Church, we miss this guidepost of the Lord.

Another place we can show devotion by giving is in the support of special ministries. These include individuals such as missionaries, media ministries, traveling ministers, evangelists or prophets who minister to the broader Church. Such giving/sowing brings about a greater harvest.

Some brethren of the Church have been endowed with a special gift for giving. These Christians learn to make money in order to give. R. A. Laidlow of New Zealand was such a man. He promised the Lord he would give more than a tithe when his income reached a certain level. When that was fulfilled, he made another covenant with the Lord to give a certain amount when his income increased to another level. He kept raising his giving and Lord kept raising his income.

He started a mail-order business and became a very wealthy man. When a need arose in the kingdom, he could write checks for large amounts and give them. If missionaries needed cars, he bought them.

He wrote a small booklet explaining the gospel called The Reason Why, which he distributed to his employees. Hundreds of thousands of copies have been printed since. Though he has gone to be with the Lord, his sowing goes on through his little booklet and his testimony as a giver lives on as an encouragement to others.

Praying

But when ye pray, use not vain repetitions, as the heathen do: for they think that they shall be heard for their much speaking.

Matthew 6:7 NKLV

If the Father knows what we need before we ask, why pray? Why not just sit back and let Him provide all we need? Because God has given man free will to choose his own way. That includes meeting his basic needs. Asking God shows dependence upon him.

Cain was determined to meet all his needs apart from God. He even insulted God by offering the fruits of his own labor as a sacrifice, knowing full well that it took a lamb's blood to gain acceptance. When confronted with the error of his ways by brother, Abel he rose up in anger and slew him. God cursed the ground so Cain could no longer support himself. God's punishment was to press home the fact that man can do nothing by himself. Cain adamantly refused to acknowledge God's help and went out from the presence of God. He never repented.

Since the Father has given us free choice, he wants us to ask so he can bless us. When we ask, we acknowledge our dependence on him. He delights to shower us with good things. We don't have to beg with much speaking, as the heathen, but he is waiting to hear the least whisper.

Of course, prayer consists of more than just asking for things. Sometimes it is just acknowledging who God is and appreciating him, communing with him, thanking him. Prayer in essence is talking to God and hearing a response.

Power for work in the Kingdom of God comes by prayer. Having given men free will, prayer becomes a legal function. If we ask God to interfere in the affairs of men, he has a legal will in which to act, ours. However, we must be careful not to presume the exact action he should take. Only he knows the best way to bless the object of our prayer. He will not answer prayers that are out of his will. If we ask amiss, to interfere in another's life, demonic powers may try to answer them.

When we intercede for others, we give God an avenue to directly bless their lives in a way they may never ask for themselves. Praying about a situation can also allow God's power to be in force instead of Satan's. When we bind the strong man of the enemy, it binds the power of Satan and the people in the situation are freed to receive God's action without interference. This sometimes takes time. Daniel prayed for three weeks, seeking the Lord concerning revelation. When a vision came at last, the angel in the vision told Daniel he responded to his prayer immediately, but a rival prince of darkness withstood him until Michael, the arch angel, came to his aid (Dan. 10:12,13). The spiritual warfare took place in the unseen world while Daniel waited.

Binding and loosing is the key to resisting Satan in the spiritual realm. Satan can be behind certain oppressions by inspiring evil men against us. Jesus told His disciples, "Men ought always to pray, and not to faint;" He told them the parable of the widow and the unjust judge (Luke 18:1-8). The woman asked for vengeance against those who wronged her. Even an unjust judge answered her request because of her persistence, just to get rid of her. But God already wants to avenge his servants. Yet He sometimes waits until the oppressor's sin is full before he acts. It requires faith on our part to wait; knowing the answer will come in time.

Jesus often went aside to pray. Sometimes he took his disciples with him. It was while he was praying that he was transfigured (Luke 9:28). On other occasions, because they saw the power it affected in his life, the disciples ask Jesus to teach them how to pray. His response was what we call the Lord's prayer, even though he intended it to be the believer's prayer.

The Lord's Prayer

This prayer is a form. The disciples ask the Lord how to pray and he gave them a pattern. Yet we take this form and pray it as if it were the whole prayer. At best it could only be very general and general prayers do little to inspire faith. It is the specific answers that cause us to marvel at God and revere him. Only when we put specifics into this prayer does it become effective in producing faith. God answers specific prayers.

The form begins with a salutation: "Our Father which art in heaven." This salutation affirms our relationship to him. He is our Father and the source of our provision.

It also recognizes that all our resources come from heaven. His Word and sovereign will rule over the very elements of earth. Realizing this in truth creates in us an attitude of humility, which must precede any enactment of this law. Blessed are the poor in spirit, for theirs is the kingdom of heaven.

"Hallowed be thy name," recognizes him as our Father. He is the high and mighty one who dwells in the high and holy place. He is the self-existent one, Jehovah/Yahwey, the great "I AM." He is also our Savior whom we love and cherish. By putting these words into the prayer form, Jesus made a place for us to tell our Father what we think of Him; a place for praise and worship in the beginning of our prayer. Because of who he is, let all the earth hallow Him now!

"Thy kingdom come, thy will be done in earth as it is in heaven." The tense of this in the original language is imperative—a command with the implication of, do it now! This part of the prayer is God's business. Jesus is asking us to be in agreement with God in the earth. Actually, it is the only type of prayer that will be answered anyway. We know this because John tells us:

> **"And this is the confidence that we have in him, that, if we ask anything according to his will, he heareth us: And if we know that he hear us, whatever we ask, we know that we have the petitions that we desired of him."**
>
> **1 John 5:14,15 AV**

Since he does not even hear prayers prayed out of his will, it is fruitless to pray any other way. In this section of the prayer, we pray about God's interests. We pray for his will in our lives, in our family, in our church fellowship, in others, in ministries, in missionaries; his will in nations, binding and loosing the powers that be, both on earth and in heaven. In short, we pray for his kingdom to come in all the earth, for rebellion to be put down and for his peace to rule as it does in heaven.

The next three sections of the prayer are personal. "Give us this day our daily bread." Here is the place to ask God for your present needs, especially those regarding your physical existence—bread, clothing, shelter, or whatever the present need. Bread, of course, will be needed again tomorrow. Give us our daily bread--provide our basic needs daily. This meets the needs of the body in the present. God knows we have need of these things before we ask. He designed us this way. By asking, we acknowledge dependence, unlike Cain who refused to give God any credit for his provision. Again, the attitude of humility is shown.

"And forgive us our debts, as we forgive our debtors," speaks to the past. Whatever is past is past and can never be undone. It can only be forgiven. This part of the prayer is directed toward our spirits, specifically our consciences. First, we forgive others who have wronged us to free our souls of bitterness, realizing we ourselves are in need of forgiveness from the Father. Again, this calls for a spirit of humility. Only a haughty spirit would expect God to forgive him without him having to forgive others. Actually, this is the only conditional part of the prayer. God cannot forgive us if we do not forgive others.

Why? Because God extends grace only to the humble. *He always resists the proud.* When we refuse to forgive, we are trying to inflict punishment, making ourselves a judge over the offender. When we do, we usurp God's place. As a result. it destroys our clear conscience and our peace, because God will not forgive us.

"And lead us not into temptation, but deliver us from evil" speaks about the future and specifically to the soul. Why do I say that? Because it is the will that chooses our way and the will is part of the soul. In this part of the prayer, we are giving our future direction into the leadership of God. We are specifically asking Him to take us by his way so we don't get caught up in snares or deceived by the enemy.

We can learn obedience by just following God's word as suggested by the Proverbs. Listen to the wisdom here:

> **For the LORD gives wisdom; From His mouth come knowledge and understanding; He stores up sound wisdom for the upright;**
>
> **Proverbs 2:6, 7 NKJV**

We learn this wisdom from godly parents. Abel learned God's way from Adam and Eve. But Cain chose to go his own way. When we go our own way we walk in rebellion and Satan can set snares anywhere. In this part of the prayer we are asking God to lead us around the snares and teach us gently so we don't need to find out things the hard way. God is able to guide us this way because: "[His] is the kingdom, and the power and the glory forever. Amen."

God always controls with almighty power. That means that Satan can only act where God allows it. If we don't pray and ask God to go before us, we may fall into a snare we can't see in the natural. It is presumption to think we can do without his help. Therefore, Jesus said ask him to guide your future steps and he will.

I experienced the wisdom of God in this manner recently. I had an "iffy" situation in the steering of my car. I took it to a repair shop voicing that I thought it could be low on power steering fluid. The mechanic confirmed my suspicions and refilled the reservoir. I had a scheduled minor outpatient operation at a distant hospital and need confidence in my car. We drove that day without any consequences.

However, two days later, when I had a follow up appointment, in returning home, I was in the middle of a busy city street when I noticed a stiffness in the steering wheel. I had prayed that morning for the Lord's wisdom in driving, since I still had a nagging worry about my car. The more I tested my steering, the more I became convinced something was wrong. I was about two blocks from a friend's auto repair shop so I decided to have the car checked again. When I went to make the wheel turn, I knew it was bad, because my power steering was completely gone. It was all I could do to make the turn.

It turned out that the main serpentine belt that turned major parts of my auto had shredded, but the Lord got me to a safe place before it broke completely. Praying about the future keeps you in many ways, even to preserving your car until the right time and place.

This concludes the prayer-form Jesus gave. Every need can be covered. You simply insert them at the proper place. It can be a prayer of supplication or intercession, according to the emphasis. Jesus never taught anything impractical or complicated. The prayer is concise and direct, covering all the basic needs. Learn to pray a prayer, instead of the pattern and you will see the faithfulness of God as he answers. You will also learn faithfulness as you develop this habit of seeking him.

Fasting

Moreover when ye fast, be not, as the hypocrites, of a sad countenance: for they disfigure their faces, that they may appear unto men to fast. Verily I say unto you, They have their reward.

Mathew 6: 16 AV

Fasting is an exercise in self-control. It cleanses the body, afflicts the soul and opens the spirit. Freed from the daily chore of digesting, fasting allows the inner body to cleanse itself from toxic materials accumulated inside. Those who fast at regular intervals, rest their internal digestive tract. This is good for the overall health of the individual. It gives the body a chance to play "catch up" before another load of food is dumped into it. Some feel fasting one day in seven produces a healthier body.

But perhaps a more important aspect of fasting is the work it accomplishes in the soul. To deprive the emotions of the delights of food is downright affliction. If you do not believe it, just try to go without food for an extended time. Or go on a restricted diet, where only the bare essentials are eaten. Then all manner of goodies come to mind. Depriving oneself of food is far harder on the soul than on the body! The lust of the flesh and the lust of the eyes both act upon the will, clamoring for fulfillment. To deliberately choose not to eat for a specific time truly curbs the flesh and gives you more control over it. At the same time, it denotes your desire to put the world aside and seek after God. This is an act of devotion.

Having quieted the bodily functions and put down the flesh, the spirit becomes more sensitive to God. Thus what might have been whispers from the Holy Spirit now become almost audible. All functions of the spirit increase. The Word of God becomes the daily bread and the Spirit living water. On special occasions, when seeking God for a specific something, men have often fasted for forty days and nights. Jesus, Himself, fasted forty days during His temptation. These long fasts are probably not what Jesus referred to in this law but rather a regular fast.

Proper Posture for Fasting

But you, when you fast, anoint your head and wash your face, so that you do not appear to men to be fasting, but to your Father who is in the secret place; and your Father who sees in secret will reward you openly.

Matthew 6:17, 18 NKJV

This is exactly opposite to the practice the Jews carried over from the Old Testament. When a man fasted in olden times, he covered his head with ashes, blackening his face and dressed himself in sackcloth. (Sackcloth was the common weave made from black goat's hair and used for tent material for the desert dwellers.) Those who fasted in the Old Testament made spectacles of themselves so everyone would know they were fasting. Mordecai embarrassed Esther by his fasting, but he got her attention (Esther 4:1).

Fasting in the New Testament focuses on getting God's attention. It is not for showing off, but for sowing righteousness. Therefore, it can only be accomplished in secret.

When no one knows but you what you have asked God for, or given to Him, or how you have restricted the flesh in order to get closer to Him, the answers and rewards are precious because "you know that you know" God did it. That increases faith. When you develop these practices as habits, it assures your faithfulness to Him. You show your devotion by such behavior

11

Lust Versus Trust: The Law of Acquisition

This law provides for the necessities of life, our attitude toward what we do for a living. It corresponds to two of the Old Testament commandments: Thou shalt not steal and Thou shalt not covet. Both of these laws deal with what belongs to others. What others have acquired through legal means we have no right to take. It follows then that there are right and wrong ways to acquire goods. Therefore, we need to know the proper way. Jesus begins this commandment with a contrast.

> "Do not lay up for yourselves treasures on earth, where moth and rust destroy and where thieves break in and steal; but lay up for yourselves treasures in heaven, where neither moth nor rust destroys and where thieves do not break in and steal. treasure is, there your heart will be also."
>
> Matthew 6:19-21 NKJV

The focus and condition of your heart determines your philosophy of life. If it is focused on the natural and in the flesh, all acquisition will be toward accumulation in this world. It will be driven by the lust of the eyes and never satisfied. It will also be fraught with worry lest someone steal your treasures. The story is told of a man whose priceless art collection burned to the ground. As he looked on the ashes his words were, "Free at last."

The problem with riches and priceless treasures is that they often possess us rather than the other way around. Greed, a grievous and spirit inspired sin, becomes a relentless pursuit of acquisition.

But if your heart has treasures in heaven, money and things become tools by which you increase your heavenly treasure. You possess your goods. They do not possess you. You are only a steward, possessions belong to God anyway, and so it depends on your point of view.

Since money buys the freedom to go anywhere or do anything, anyone can be tempted to seek money to support sin. The "be" attitude here is mourning. A man who curbs his natural appetites and limits the lust of his eyes can trust God to care for his needs. Unbridled appetites, lust for things and power lead to all manner of sins. On the other hand, a temperate man can live comfortably, if he is willing to work hard to earn his way and trust God to meet his needs. If he lets God supply his desires, God will reward him by giving him the desires of his heart. This brings a life of peace and great contentment.

Heart Chooses

Mammon	God
(Temporary)	Wealth in Heaven
If stored cam be Destroyed by decay, thieves, moths, or natural disaster.	(Eternal) Indestructible Untarnished Given By Faith (when needed).

Diagramming this contrast, we can see that what makes the difference is this: if we truly *know* God, we *know* we can trust Him. That faith makes a difference in how we look at possessions. Then money and things become tools in the kingdom of God. When holding this kind of attitude, God is free to bless us with *all* things that we need.

Proper Ways to Acquire Wealth

In the book of Proverbs, Wisdom personified says:

> "I, wisdom, dwell with prudence, And find out knowledge and discretion. The fear of the LORD is to hate evil; Pride and arrogance and the evil way.
>
> And the perverse mouth I hate. Counsel is mine, and sound wisdom; I am understanding, I have strength. By me kings reign, And rulers decree justice. By me princes rule, and nobles, All the judges of the earth. I love those who love me,
>
> And those who seek me diligently will find me.
>
> Riches and honor are with me, Enduring riches and righteousness. My fruit is better than gold, yes, than fine gold,
>
> And my revenue than choice silver. I traverse the way of righteousness, In the midst of the paths of justice, That I may cause those who love me to inherit wealth, That I may fill their treasuries.
>
> **Proverbs 8:12-21 NKJV**

The first prerequisite to wealth is acquiring wisdom, since through it God dispenses wealth.

Wisdom can be defined as knowledge and understanding that lead to good judgment when making decisions. Therefore, to obtain wisdom one must first acquire knowledge with understanding.

The first knowledge is to know what God expects from a man in righteousness and integrity. He must know that God honors truth, honesty, and faithfulness to one's word and *diligence*.⁵

God forbids theft, embezzlement and fraud. This understanding prepares one for an honest pursuit of wealth. Jeremiah 17:11 says: "As a partridge that broods but does not hatch, so is he who gets riches, but not by right; It will leave him in the midst of his days, And at his end he will be a fool."

So a man needs to know what is right and make his living in view of this knowledge. Then he must prepare himself for a certain vocation by learning first the knowledge and then the skill necessary to perform it. Applying diligence and wisdom will bring wealth, even to those who do not trust God. (Wealth here is defined as having a surplus of one's needs. But leaving God out will bring all the temptations associated with wealth.) *Those who do not learn do not earn.* I passed a sign one day that read: "Failing to prepare is preparing to fail."

Colleges and universities prepare people for all types of careers, but knowledge does not have to be of the book kind. Highly skilled laborers learn their trade through apprentice programs. Labor unions often provide such schooling, or Technical schools that teach hands-on skills. Paul, the mighty man of God, was a tentmaker (making prayer shawls). That was his occupational skill, but he also had a spiritual schooling at the feet of Gamaliel, a great teacher of the law in Israel. Paul is a good example of what Christians in the kingdom of God should be. All should

---

⁵ A lazy man can never find wealth in God or the world. Proverbs 18:19; 19:15, 24; 20:4; 21:25; 22:13.

have a vocation to earn a living and it should be coupled with a spiritual knowledge of the Word.

Poverty is Often an Eye Problem

> "The lamp of the body is the eye. If therefore your eye is good, your whole body will be full of light. But if your eye is bad, your whole body will be full of darkness. If therefore the light that is in you is darkness, how great is that darkness! "No one can serve two masters; for either he will hate the one and love the other, or else he will be loyal to the one and despise the other. You cannot serve God and mammon.
>
> **Matthew 6:22-24 NKJV**

A blind man in Scripture is a spiritual picture of a man without some essential knowledge, since light speaks of truth. If the eyes of our understanding are darkened, we are said to be blind, making us incapable of receiving light. The problem with the poor man is not blindness but lack of focus.

The problem here seems to be double-mindedness. If the eyes do not function together they bring a blurred vision, because they are not both focused on the same thing. If we have one eye on God and one eye on riches, we have cockeyed vision. James 1 tells us that a double-minded man can expect nothing from God. Experience tells us that neither can a double-minded man in the world accomplish anything.

On the other hand, a man who decides to make a million by the time he reaches thirty-five focuses his total being on his goal and often meets it. Why? *Because he is totally focused.*

Therefore, to acquire wealth, whether it is physical or spiritual, one must be focused.

We will focus on one of two masters. We will serve God or we will serve Mammon, which is simply earning money for the sake of having money.

Poverty brings other problems with it. Envy or worry will fill the man who lacks what he needs—envy if he looks at others' possessions or worry about meeting his own needs. Trust in God's provision eliminates worry, which is just the opposite of trust.

Jesus said:

> No one can serve two masters; for either he will hate the one and love the other, or else he will be loyal to the one and despise the other. You cannot serve God and mammon.
>
> "Therefore I say to you, do not worry about your life, what you will eat or what you will drink; nor about your body, what you will put on. Is not life more than food and the body more than clothing? Look at the birds of the air, for they neither sow nor reap nor gather into barns; yet your heavenly Father feeds them. Are you not of more value than they? Which of you by worrying can add one cubit to his stature?
>
> "So why do you worry about clothing? Consider the lilies of the field, how they grow: they neither toil nor spin; and yet I say to you that even Solomon in all his glory was not arrayed like one of these. Now if God so clothes the grass of the field, which today is, and tomorrow is thrown into the oven, will He not much more clothe you, O you of little faith?

> "Therefore do not worry, saying, 'What shall we eat?' or 'What shall we drink?' or 'What shall we wear?' For after all these things the Gentiles seek. For your heavenly Father knows that you need all these things.
>
> But seek first the kingdom of God and His righteousness, and all these things shall be added to you. Therefore do not worry about tomorrow, for tomorrow will worry about its own things. Sufficient for the day is its own trouble.
>
> **Matthew 6: 25-34 NKJV**

This entire passage boils down to this: *Do not worry.* Trust God for your needs. We quote Jim Elliot again, one of the five missionaries killed by the Auca Indians. He said, "A man is no fool to give up what he cannot keep, in order to gain what he cannot lose." That is a statement of wisdom. Things, things, things! The world is obsessed with things. Jesus said it all when He said, "What does it profit a man, if he gain the whole world and lose his own soul." Things will never satisfy unless they come as blessings from God. Paul says it well:

> If anyone teaches otherwise and does not consent to wholesome words, even the words of our Lord Jesus Christ, and to the doctrine which accords with godliness, he is proud, knowing nothing, but is obsessed with disputes and arguments over words, from which come envy, strife, reviling, evil suspicions, useless wrangling of men of corrupt minds and destitute of the truth, who suppose that godliness is a means of gain. From such withdraw yourself [prosperity teachers?] Now godliness with contentment is great gain. For we brought nothing into this world, and it is certain we can carry nothing out. And having food and clothing, with

these we shall be content. But those who desire to be rich fall into temptation and a snare, and into many foolish and harmful lusts which drown men in destruction and perdition. For the love of money is a root of all kinds of evil, for which some have strayed from the faith in their greediness, and pierced themselves through with many sorrows.

I Timothy 6:6-10 NKJV

If we trust God daily for our needs and trust our desires for the future to Him, a life of contentment follows. Self-control or temperance comes with it as well. The constant lusting of the flesh and the eyes destroys temperance, but *seeking first* the Kingdom of God adds all things that we need. What a tremendous blessing—health, wealth, wisdom *and contentment* all come with the fruit of temperance.

12

Critique Versus Unique: The Law of Criticism

In any natural society the people engage in a harsh process of mutual appraisal. Glenn Tinder, in his book *The Political Meaning Of Christianity* says: "People are ceaselessly judged and ranked, and in turn they ceaselessly judge and rank others. . . . It is partly a struggle for self-esteem; we judge ourselves, for the most part, as others judge us. . . . we anxiously strive to evade the adverse judgments of others, but we are inclined to subject others to our own harsh judgment." It is to this problem of society that the law of Criticism applies.

This law produces the fruit of long-suffering through the attitude of mercy. Since all in any society are fraught with inadequacies and weaknesses, no one can afford to put another down without spotlighting his own fallibility. This is exactly what the law says:

> **Judge not, that you be not judged. For with what judgment you judge, you will be judged; and with the measure you use, it will be measured back to you. And why do you look at the speck in your brother's eye, but do not consider the plank in your own eye? Or how can you say to your brother, 'Let me remove the speck from your eye'; and look, a plank is in your own eye? Hypo-**

> **crite! First remove the plank from your own eye, and then you will see clearly to remove the speck from your brother's eye.**
>
> **Matthew 7:1-5 NKJV**

According to this law, judging is an eye problem. (Here the eye speaks of perception.) We can never rate other people as they truly deserve to be rated, because we cannot see enough of their lives. The log in our own eye may simply consist of preoccupation with our own lives; or it may consist of fallacies in our own perception, clouded by prejudice or false information. Then again it may be due to the perspective of our viewing.

Seen from the view in the eyes of the seer, the speck in another person seems large. But remember, even a speck in the eye of the seer blocks out a great deal of the picture, we cannot truly critique the lives of others. Therefore, the law says, don't judge at all; instead, develop a live-and-let-live attitude. This attitude proves to be a unique stance in the world of judgmental people. "Blessed are the merciful, for they shall obtain mercy."

This view does not mean we turn a blind eye to our responsibilities. For instance, parents will still need to rate the characters of their children for correction. Pastors still need to discern the needs of their congregations for correction. Legal judges must still dispense judgment according to the laws. This law aims mainly at society in general and personal relationships in particular.

Gaps

Peter Lord, a popular conference speaker, preaches that the problems we have with other people are all due to "gaps." Funk & Wagnall's World Dictionary defines gap as "an opening or parting in anything." Webster defines gap as: "an opening made by breaking or parting—a blank space—a lag—a disparity (unequal)." But in the context of our discussion, Peter Lord defines gap as the distance between what is, as opposed to what ought to be. Bill Gothard illustrates this concept by a disagreement between a wife and her husband. The husband sees his problem from how far he has already come in overcoming it. His wife looks at how far he still has to go. The difference is a gap, which Bill Gothard labels as a blind spot. We are all "short of the glory of God," full of blind spots, full of gaps. The law states, "You hypocrite" first get rid of your own gaps before you try to rid someone else of theirs. Hear what Peter Lord says about gaps:

1. Gaps are easy to see.
2. Gaps are easy to judge.
3. Gaps are even easier to misjudge.
4. Gaps cannot be filled in by another person.

How we handle these "gaps" in others determines the development of longsuffering in us. We have two examples in the Scriptures: Jesus, the Advocate, who intercedes for the brethren, and Satan, the Accuser of the brethren. We will emulate either one or the other.

When the Pharisees brought to Jesus the woman caught in adultery, He did not accuse her in her weakness. Neither did he condemn her although she was evidently guilty as charged. He realized that she was a victim in his conflict with the Pharisees. Instead, he simply asked that the one without sin throw the *first* stone. That eliminated her accusers. Matthew quotes a Scripture in Isaiah that was fulfilled in Jesus: "A bruised reed shall he not break and a smoking flax shall he not quench" (Matthew 12:20). Jesus states in another place that he came not to judge but to save. Therefore, he allowed the bruised reed, the woman, to be bruised, and he did not break her. He is our example. We are to do the same. Jude says that even Gabriel, the archangel, durst not bring a railing accusation against Satan (Jude 9).

In another situation the disciples, mainly Judas, upbraided Mary for breaking the expensive ointment on her master's head. Jesus quickly came to Mary's rescue, saying, "Let her alone. She has done a good thing." Again, He is our example. We can do the same when someone condemns another.

What can we do about those blatant "gaps" in others? Answer: Suffer them over a long time! Meanwhile, we can go into our closets and pray for the fault-ridden like Jesus does. Another solution might be to address the problem rather than condemning the person. Paul instructing Timothy says:

> **But avoid foolish and ignorant disputes, knowing that they generate strife. And a servant of the Lord must not quarrel but be gentle to all, able to teach, patient, in humility correcting those who are in opposition, if God perhaps will grant them repentance, so that they may know the truth, and that they may come to their senses and escape the snare of the devil, having been taken captive by him to do his will.**
>
> 2 Timothy 2:24-26 NKJV

Foolish and unlearned questions do not come from gentle and submissive spirits, but from ones filled with "gaps." Paul tells Timothy to be kind and patient and willing to teach about the problems in question. Adopting a meek attitude removes the defensive posture of the one opposing and allows him to see the problem in himself without receiving condemnation. It is the attitude of mercy that disarms him and makes him willing to hear. On the other hand, if we condemn a man by harsh judgments, he immediately puts up a defense and reciprocates with judgment.

So, the answer to the question of handling "gaps" in others is longsuffering and prayer just like Christ, or patient and gentle exposure of the problem without showing condemnation.

Satan delights to shoot fiery darts. Since words wound, they become weapons of the spirit world. But Satan, being a spirit himself, can only inspire them to come through mortal beings. Therefore, if we give in to judgmental words, we serve his cause. Both Old Testament and New Testament law forbids evil-speaking which consists of curses, condemnations and untruths. Satan shot his fiery darts at Jesus through the Pharisees. They judged Him by their pre-set religious convictions. They said, "You are blaspheming" (Matthew 26:65; 9:3). "You cast out devils by Beelzebub, the prince of demons" (Luke 11:18). "We be not born of fornication" implies that Jesus was a bastard (John 8:41). "Thou hast a demon" (John 7:20; 8:48; 8:52). They called Him "gluttonous and a winebibber" (Matthew 11:19). When the Pharisees accused and judged Jesus, it was from spite, envy and prejudiced information. But when Jesus accused, He spoke the truth and convicted them.

A judge in the Old Testament decided cases between disputing parties. He was usually elderly, one people trusted as a wise man, one full of life's experiences and well able to arbitrate their differences. Usually several men served in this capacity at the city gate. Theirs was a position of honor and respect. Lawyers among the Levites also judged the people (Deuteronomy. 17:9).

In the New Testament, Jesus encountered a portion of the Pharisees who were specifically lawyers. This special branch of the priests decided questions of the Jewish law. Jesus constantly resisted their narrow interpretations and additions of tradition. He pointed out that they doted on the letter of the law, tithing the small items such as herbs, but neglected the spirit of the law that administered judgment and mercy (Matthew 23:23).

Judging others from our own convictions implies that we know all about the law (in our case how to live the proper way). It says to him, *"I have a right to judge you, since I am superior to you. Therefore, you should receive the judgment I give to improve yourself!"*

Human nature resists this criticism, especially when a spirit of superiority abounds in the one doing the judging. Immediately, the one being judged looks at the judge to see if he or she is qualified—and promptly decrees his own judgment of the judge. Since no one is perfect, unsolicited judgment merely invokes more judgment. The law of sowing and reaping comes into effect. A man will reap what he sows. If I judge another, I myself will be judged.

We are destined to judge the world to come (1 Corinthians. 6:2), and we should judge disputes as a body in the Church even now. Yet the right to judge another individually is not ours. James says:

> **Do not speak evil of one another, brethren. He who speaks evil of a brother and judges his brother, speaks**

> evil of the law and judges the law. But if you judge the law, you are not a doer of the law but a judge. There is one Lawgiver who is able to save and to destroy. Who are you to judge another?
>
> **James 4:11, 12 NKJV**

Who are you, a judge? No. You cannot save, but Satan can certainly use you to destroy. Since a person often derives his own self-worth from others' assessments of him, harsh judgments destroy self-esteem, relationships and productivity.

Paul addresses another reason why men try to judge: the difference in understanding the Word of God. A weak Christian may have set up certain rules to follow to keep himself pure and on the right track. He has trained his conscience accordingly. But he sees you participating in something his conscience condemns. He immediately wants to judge that you are sinning. On the other hand, perhaps you, having a little more knowledge of the Word, understand that what you do does not contradict the Word, but only his conscience. Your tendency would be to discount him as an inferior brother. Both judgments are wrong. Paul, addressing this problem says:

> **Who are you to judge another's servant? To his own master he stands or falls. Indeed, he will be made to stand, for God is able to make him stand. . . . .**
>
> **But why do you judge your brother? Or why do you show contempt for your brother? For we shall all stand before the judgment seat of Christ. For it is written: "As I live, says the LORD, Every knee shall bow to Me, And every tongue shall confess to God]**

> So then each of us shall give account of himself to God.
>
> **Romans Romans 14:4; 10-12 NKJV**

Bob Mumford, popular charismatic teacher, bemoans about Christians who run around everywhere wrecking havoc, "playing sheriff" in the kingdom of God. The exposure of faults changes nothing and causes a great deal of ill will. Only the Holy Ghost can convict, and therefore, change an individual.

Since we are a people fraught with weaknesses and shortcomings, our attitude toward others must be one of mercy. Armed with this attitude and a determination to remove the log from our own eye, we will gradually learn to exercise patience with the faults and weaknesses of others and produce the fruit of longsuffering. This fruit is different from patience so often substituted in modern translations, it literally means to suffer someone's fault for a long time.

13

Knowing Versus "Blowing"
The Law of Understanding

This, the last law of righteousness, preserves the fruit of joy, and goes with the attitude of hunger toward the Word of God. Therefore, the law deals with a synopsis of using the Scriptures (especially these laws) in our daily lives. This many-faceted list adds or subtracts joy:

How not to share spiritual jewels.
How to receive from God.
How to treat others.
Where to walk in life brings joy of life
Who to follow in the kingdom preserves joy.
How to serve God's using his gifts—Joy!
How to stand.

How not to Share and with Whom

Do not give what is holy to the dogs; nor cast your pearls before swine, lest they trample them under their feet, and turn and tear you in pieces.

Matthew 7:6 NKJV

Since no one would cast the Word or anything else considered holy before dogs or swine, we have to assume he uses a metaphor rather than speaking literally. Therefore, we need to establish what he means by pearls, dogs and swine. Scripture uses these terms as similes.

The Scriptures lists pearls among the most precious things of the earth, treasured by all. In the parable of the pearl of great price, the possessor gained rights to enter into the heavenly city through one of the gates made of one pearl (Rev. 22:14). However, in this case the pearl was probably accounted a particular treasure of the individual, such as some new spiritual truth given him by the Holy Spirit. Such a treasure would not be appreciated by a non-spiritual person.

Looking to the general use of dogs, we find that in Scripture they cleaned up: eating garbage and crumbs under the table; devouring the slain in the battlefield along with birds of prey; licking the blood of Ahab, and eating Jezebel. Men used dogs for watchmen, but unfaithful human watchmen were called dumb dogs. God would not receive the hire of a whore or the price of a dog into the house of the Lord to pay for a vow. God told Gideon not to choose men who lapped like a dog when drinking water. David, when speaking to Saul, compared himself to a dead dog, a flea. From these uses we understand that the Scriptures hold the dog in low esteem.

This concept is further strengthened when we see how they used them in metaphors. In Psalm 22:16 speaking prophetically as Christ on the cross, David says, "For dogs have compassed me: the assembly of the wicked have enclosed me. Here the wicked are equated to dogs. Remember, the Pharisees watched Him die, so they may be indicated here. Isaiah compares unfaithful shepherds to "greedy dogs" (Isa. 56:11). In Philippians 3:2 Paul calls evil workers of the Jews "dogs." Peter compares "dogs" to the false teachers in the Church, which bring in damnable heresies. Revelation 22:15 includes "dogs" in the same category with sorcerers, whoremongers, and murderers who are outside the gates of paradise. From these uses we draw the conclusion that "dogs," besides being the lowest of creatures, represent false religious workers who do not know Christ intimately.

How many times have I wasted a morning trying to share spiritual truth with Jehovah's Witnesses, only to end up frustrated and feeling like a failure as God's witness. What a complete loss of joy! Of course, one must discern whether you are dealing with new convert or a hardened, seasoned JW. Once in awhile, you can reach them. God will lead you. He knows whose hearts are open to receive him and whose are closed.

Jehovah's Witnesses are not the only ones in this classification. Any religious person who does not know Christ and insists on teaching others would qualify. Because of their own teaching, they are unable to hear you. Leading an unbeliever to Christ brings joy. Great joy breaks out in heaven over one single convert to the Lord. But Jesus says don't expect to find joy when sharing with "dogs." In fact, He says don't do it.

Now let's look at swine; how are they used in Scripture metaphorically? First of all, the pig is an unclean animal (as is the dog), but the pig was also used as a sacrificial animal to the heathen idols. This made it twice as abominable. Its nature was to wallow in the mire. Also, it could be dangerous because of the razor-sharp tusks. This animal contrasts to a sheep in metaphor. The unclean sow can be washed, dressed with a ribbon and perfumed, but left on its own, it will return to wallowing in the mire, because that is its true nature. This pictures the natural flesh. In contrast sheep are compared to believers in Scripture. The nature of a sheep is to love green pastures and still waters. They can get dirty, but they don't like it. The demons asked to enter swine when Jesus cast them out of the Gadarene demoniac, showing their affinity to them.

Casting our pearls in the path of the unsaved or unlearned takes away joy, because spiritual things are foolishness to them. They not only do not appreciate them, but some also will not appreciate you for sharing them.

How to Receive

> Ask, and it will be given to you; seek, and you will find; knock, and it will be opened to you. For everyone who asks receives, and he who seeks finds, and to him who knocks it will be opened. Or what man is there among you who, if his son asks for bread, will give him a stone? Or if he asks for a fish, will he give him a serpent? If you then, being evil, know how to give good gifts to your children, how much more will your Father who is in heaven give good things to those who ask Him!
>
> **Matthew 7: 7-11 NKJV**

Receiving from God comes in three forms: asking for something, seeking, a result of looking for something, and knocking, a result of persistent determination to get past an obstacle by opening something that is closed. Joy comes as a result of receiving these requests. In John 16:24 Jesus told His disciples, "Hitherto have ye ask nothing in my name, ask; that your joy may be full." When one of my sons was a teenager, he got all excited when God answered one of his prayers specifically. He said, "Why didn't you tell me how exciting it is to pray?" Joy!

God delights to give us our needs when we depend on Him. Jesus said if we who are evil give good gifts to our children how much more shall our heavenly Father give good gifts to us. He goes a bit further in Luke where he says, "How much more shall your heavenly Father give the Holy Spirit to them that ask him?" Joy! What shall we ask for? First, we should ask for our daily needs as told us in the Lord's pattern for prayer. Second, we should ask for forgiveness for our sins. Third, we should ask for direction for the future. These are basic and all mentioned in the Lord's Prayer.

But beyond our personal needs, we can ask for others' needs. We can ask for God's will to be known in others' lives. We can ask for wisdom. We can ask for God's will to be done on earth. We can ask for demons to be bound. Asking for things to consume upon our lust is asking amiss, but James says we have not because we ask not (James 4:2,3).

Actually, we don't need to ask for personal desires. God has already promised to give us the desires of our heart if we truly serve him. He knows our heart, so he already knows the needs.

Receiving as a result of asking shows a single-minded faith in God and his answers bring great joy. However, in order to successfully receive answers to our asking, we must ask in accordance to God's will, found in the Scriptures.

Seeking is different from asking. When we seek something, we go after it. In the parables Jesus taught about three seekers. The shepherd sought the sheep that was lost.

The woman sought the coin that was lost. The father sought the son that was lost. In each instance, when that which was lost was found, the seeker asked his friends to rejoice with him. Joy! Therefore, one thing we seek after is the lost. When we win the lost to God, great joy breaks out in heaven. We also enter into the Father's joy. In fact, there is a specific crown called the crown of rejoicing, a reward given for winning the lost and bringing them to maturity in the Lord.

Another thing we seek is a strong personal relationship with the Lord. The reason for seeking the Lord, according to Isaiah 55, is to be able to think the thoughts of God and do his ways after receiving his words. As a result "we shall go out with joy and be led forth with peace."

The Gentiles seek things. Jesus said that the adulterous generation seeks a sign. We were told in the Law of Acquisition to seek first the kingdom of God instead of the treasures of this earth. Later on in this law, we will be told to seek to enter the strait gate that leads to life. Paul told the Colossians to seek those things, which are above (Colossians 3:1). So we could say that seeking has to do with our goals. When our goals are met, it brings forth joy.

Knocking differs from asking and seeking in that the way is closed before us. An obstacle prevents the desire to be met. Knocking is asking for the removal of an obstacle that stands in the way. Knock for opportunity, perhaps for a specific service opportunity to be opened. The enemy may have closed the way before us. We knock on the closed door to get God's power to move against our enemy.

Peter was in prison. It seemed like the end of his ministry. The Christians prayed for his release and God sent an angel. The prayers knocked; the door opened. We knock to obtain deeper truth, or for the unlocking of secrets.

Daniel asked God to reveal Nebuchadnezzar's dream and the interpretation thereof. The dream itself was a secret—not even Nebuchadnezzar himself could remember it. This was a knocking. Wherefore, Daniel stated that God was the revealer of secrets. Later, Daniel, after reading the prophecies of Jeremiah and understanding the limit of the Israelites' stay in Babylon, prayed for God to restore Jerusalem and the temple as He had promised. As a result, Gabriel was sent to help Daniel understand the whole future of Israel, by giving him the vision of the seventy weeks.

Daniel had "set his face" to seek the Lord by prayer, fasting with sackcloth and ashes. This prayer implies persistence, a sticking with it, until the opening comes. This is the essence of knocking.

When I was first saved, I was fascinated with prophecy and particularly the book of Revelation. I set my mind to understand it. For two or three years I studied and studied, but it remained mostly a mystery. I read other commentaries and discovered conflict among writers. Finally, after persistently sticking with it, the Lord himself began to open it up to me. As a result I was able to publish a text book exposition twenty-eight years later.

Dangers in Seeking Spiritual Favors

Asking for more of the Holy Spirit has come under attack of the enemy causing some Christians to fear what they might receive. Jesus foresaw this problem and gave the answer in the midst of this law.

> Or what man is there of you, whom if his son ask bread, will he give him a stone? Or if he ask a fish, will he give him a serpent?
>
> **Matthew 7:9,10 AV**
>
> Or if he shall ask an egg, will he offer him a scorpion? If ye then, being evil, know how to give good gifts to your children: how much more shall your heavenly Father give the Holy Spirit to them that ask him?
>
> **Luke 11:12,13 AV**

Much confusion exists over what Jesus meant in these passages. It can be cleared up by asking two things: who is the giver and what are his gifts? Jesus said to the Pharisees, "Ye are of your father the devil, and the lusts of your father ye will do." If your father is the devil and you ask for spiritual gifts, you will receive the gifts he gives. When Jesus fasted in the wilderness, *who* was it who suggested that He turn stones into bread when He hungered? Satan. Daily bread for life comes from the provider of all life. Life comes from life. Turning stones to bread is a trick, an illusion skipping the life process and has no value in sustaining life.

Satan's answers are always lies or half-truths. His gifts are not life-producing. They always lead to death. Jesus' answer to Satan was: "Man shall not live by bread alone but by every word that proceedeth out of the mouth of God." In commanding the stones to be bread, He would have taken matters into His own hands—doing his own thing—without the Father.

Therefore, if one asks for the Father to provide for his physical daily needs (which bread represents), God will provide it. It will not be a stone that looks like bread but real bread that sustains life.

If he asks for fish, God, the Father will give fish. Again, who is associated with serpents? Satan. Fish represents dominion. It was the first creature God put under Adam's control. Fish were prominent in Jesus' ministry. He multiplied two fish along with the five loaves to feed the five thousand. He extracted a coin from a fish to pay taxes (Matthew 17:27; Mark 6:38). He told His disciples to put their net into the waters after they had failed to land anything all night, and they came up with a net full of fish (John 21:5, 6). In all these instances, He took dominion over the natural and performed the supernatural. He sometimes gives us dominion over the natural when the Holy Spirit uses us to perform signs and wonders.

Snakes in Scripture always portray an evil, deceptive or harmful dominion. The dark kingdom considers the serpent wise. Satan himself is portrayed as such. Therefore, the gift of a serpent could only come from the father of lies, who promises his children positions of glory and dominion through his powers. Yet because of the way they are attained they always end in destruction. If a man asks God for an egg, (an embryo of something not yet developed) the Father will not give him a scorpion.

If a man asks God for the baptism of the Holy Spirit, he will receive an explosive and growing measure of the Holy Spirit in his life. On the other hand, if a child of Satan, who is deceived to think he is a Christian, asks for the baptism of the Holy Spirit, he will receive a demonic spirit—a scorpion.

I saw an illustration of this truth when a stranger attended our charismatic Bible study one night. She apparently had asked for the baptism of the Holy Spirit without having been saved first. She continually burst out into speaking in tongues, disrupting the teacher.

Finally, discerning that the spirit behind her tongues was not of the Lord, the teacher commanded her to stop in the name of Jesus. She stopped immediately. She had received a scorpion who was trying to destroy our meeting. Did not Jesus tell His disciples that He had given them dominion over scorpions (Luke 10:17-20) equating them to evil spirits? Our teacher had done just that. He took authority over the spirit and it obeyed.

So the father of deception gives out spirits of deception masquerading as God's Spirit. Jesus gives us this understanding so we will not be confused about the gifts of the heavenly Father. We should never be afraid to ask our Father for more of the Holy Spirit. Satan is the author of this fear. He knows that if we have the power of the Holy Spirit in our lives, he will be defeated. Therefore, he generates this fear across the body of Christ to keep us from power.

The result of asking, seeking and knocking brings God's good gifts and Joy! Joy! Joy!

How to Act

Therefore all things whatsoever ye would that men should do to you, do ye even so to them: for this is the law and the prophets.

Matthew 7:12 ASV

This passage of Scripture is known as the Golden Rule, because if everyone behaved in this manner, the world would be a wonderful place.

Unfortunately, when the world quotes the Golden Rule, it is in the negative. Don't do anything to another you wouldn't want anyone to do to you. The positive form says more. If you want to receive joy, do for others what makes you happy. Under the law of sowing and reaping this, means multiplying your own happiness. You begin a chain of events by doing someone a good turn. He, in turn, having been blessed by you learns the value of blessing. Then he, having the joy of blessing from you will go on to bless others. The blessing will keep going and finally return to you. This is not a passive stance, but an active one in doing good. For who would want to receive evil? Therefore, if we want joy, we first provide it for others and it will return to us.

Another way to look at this rule might be from the point of view of each man's motivation gift. According to Romans 12:6-8, each Christian is endowed with grace in the form of a gift. This gift motivates his entire service to God.

If his gift is prophecy (speaking the truth), he will always appreciate the truth being spoken to him. If his gift is ministry (serving others), he will appreciate being served. If his gift is teaching, he will enjoy being taught. If his gift is to exhort (encourage) he will enjoy encouragement from others. If his gift is giving, he appreciates the sacrifice others make to help him. If his gift is ruling he finds joy when others help him organize a situation. And finally, if his gift is mercy, he will gladly receive mercy from others. Why do I say this? Because we all tend to do for others what we ourselves enjoy, what we are motivated to do. I myself, am a teacher. Therefore, I tend to illustrate truth to others.

Once I stood toward the front of the Church auditorium observing the ministry that was taking place. A mother with a whimpering small child was waiting for ministry. Suddenly the minister's wife came and took the child out so the mother could wait, unhampered. I stood there wondering, "Why didn't I think of that?" But it never entered my mind. I learned from watching another exercise her gift. Of mercy. Next time I will know what to do. If we all exercise our gifts to others, and let them learn how to do what comes naturally to us, what joy it will produce in all our lives.

Where to Walk

Because strait is the gate, and narrow the way, that leadeth unto life, and few there be that find it.

Matthew 7:13, 14 AV

The wide gate and the broad way have room for a crowd to travel abreast. Anything goes, because so much space makes room for the manifestation of fleshly desires of every description. The broad way reminds me of a carnival fairway lined with booths to tempt every pleasure. Hucksters of every ilk clamor for the crowd's attention. On this side is a booth of ring toss to win cheap prizes that dazzle the eye (Worldliness, the lust of the eyes). Over here is a shooting gallery and a strong man's bell where you can impress your date with your marksmanship or your strength (Pride of life). Next in line, the bingo booth appears where you might win lots of money for little investment (Love of Money, the root of all evil). Farther down the strip are the girlie shows (Lust of the flesh). Strolling through these distractions, time suddenly runs out and the Lord confronts the foolish one with a loss of time, resources, and a wasted life walking on the broad way.

On the other hand, the narrow gate appears like the turnstile of the subway where each man enters one at a time. It costs something to go on the narrow way. First of all it requires a separation from the crowd. Then one must search just to find it, because it is not easy to see.

Once discovered, it requires effort to push through the entrance. After that, the way is restricted to one path that leads to a focused end—Life, Joy and great fulfillment. The narrowness of the way restricts the flesh, because it represents the Word and makes no provision for sin. The way itself is not life, but it leads to life. Jesus said in his high priestly prayer in John 17, that eternal life is to know the only true God and Jesus Christ, whom he sent (vs. 3). Therefore, walking in the confines of the Word leads to knowing the Father and Jesus. Joy!

The broad way leaves the flesh unhindered and leads to grief, loss, and destruction of life. If we would have joy, we must walk the right way—the narrow way.

Who not to Follow

Beware of false prophets, which come to you in sheep's clothing, but inwardly they are ravening wolves.

You shall know them by their fruits. Do men gather grapes of thorns, or figs of thistles?

Even so every good tree bringeth forth good fruit; but a corrupt tree bringeth forth evil fruit. A good tree cannot bring forth evil fruit, neither can a corrupt tree bring forth good fruit.

Wherefore by their fruits ye shall know them.

Matthew 7:15-20AV

Beware of leaders whose desires are to fleece the sheep. Certainly, being fleeced kills joy, so we need to learn how to recognize such predators! On the surface they look like other Christians—sheep's clothing. But inwardly they are ravenous like wolves—rapacious, voracious, and greedy for wealth and glory. They will take your money to make a name for themselves. We have a mixed metaphor in this passage. The teachers/prophets are wolves, and the Christians are the sheep. But Jesus compares the teachers/prophets' ministries to fruits from trees.

This is where the metaphor changes from the nature of what they are like to the nature of what they produce. Both Jesus and Paul liked to compare good results to fruit. Jesus used the analogy of the vine to show production in a holy life (John 15:5).

Perhaps the reason for the particular use of grapes and figs was to show the connection to the domestic lives of the people. To be prosperous and happy domestically in the Middle-East, each family had its own vine and its own fig tree. The vine produced the grapes for wine, often equated with joy in the Scriptures, The fig tree was considered a comfort because of the shade (figs grow on trees in the Middle East), and the figs could be dried for winter. These trees contributed to the quality of life of the family.

Several years ago when we visited Israel, I was careful to notice that almost every back yard had a vine and a fig tree, so Jesus used a very common illustration, one that still exists today. This Illustration suggests that the fruit from these teachers should be of value to our everyday lives.

The good trees are varieties that produce acceptable fruit—such as our name brand varieties, for instance Navel or Valencia oranges. However, If you plant a seed from such an orange, you will get a sour orange, a corrupt tree. Acceptable fruit only grows from slips from the original tree. The same is true in ministry. Good ministries grow from other good ministries by discipleship. The apostle John talks about those who pervert the gospel as:

> **They went out from us, but they were not of us; for if they had been of us, they would no doubt have continued with us: but they went out, that they might be made manifest that they were not all of us,**
>
> *1 John 2:19.AV*

They started out as part of the Church, but they were more interested in their own way. They became seeds instead of slips, and they produce a corrupt tree with corrupt fruit. Instead of receiving good fruit from the ministry of such trees, the teachers strip their congregations of their resources.

If a man's ministry does not edify, produce joy or add comfort to one's spiritual life, it's a corrupt tree and should not be supported or followed because joy will be lost. "By their [sour] fruits ye shall know them." Jesus expands on this law:

> **For a good tree does not bear bad fruit, nor does a bad tree bear good fruit. For every tree is known by its own fruit. For men do not gather figs from thorns, nor do they gather grapes from a bramble bush.**
>
> **A good man out of the good treasure of his heart brings forth good; and an evil man out of the evil treasure of his heart brings forth evil.**

For out of the abundance of the heart his mouth speaks."But why do you call Me 'Lord, Lord,' and not do the things which I say?

Luke 6:43-46 NKLV

Continuing the same subject in Matthew:

You will know them by their fruits. Do men gather grapes from thornbushes or figs from thistles? Even so, every good tree bears good fruit, but a bad tree bears bad fruit. A good tree cannot bear bad fruit, nor can a bad tree bear good fruit. Every tree that does not bear good fruit is cut down and thrown into the fire. Therefore by their fruits you will know them.

Matthew 7: 18-20 AV

The sour fruits come out of their mouth. The thorns and thistles relate back to their natures as wolves. Since Jesus equated thorns and thistles to riches and the cares of this world (Matthew 13:22), these corrupt trees seek money and glory not the edification of the body of Christ. Of course no fruit at all comes from thorns and thistles.

How to Use the Power Gifts

"Not everyone who says to Me, 'Lord, Lord,' shall enter the kingdom of heaven, but he who does the will of My Father in heaven. Many will say to Me in that day, 'Lord, Lord, have we not prophesied in Your name, cast out demons in Your name, and done many wonders in Your name?' And then I will declare to them, 'I never knew you; depart from Me, you who practice lawlessness!'

Matthew 7:21-23 NKJV

Three significant words dominate these verses: the title of *Lord*; the Lord's description of their works—*Lawlessness;* and the person whose will must be followed by those working in His kingdom—His *Father's*.

First, he was not the Lord of these complainers. Jesus once said to a disciple, "Why call ye me Lord, Lord, and do not the things which I say" (Luke 6:47). How could the rebel call Jesus Lord when his whole agenda was his own? If one is a Lord, then he must be obeyed. The same was true of these miracle workers. It is obvious that supernatural power was involved in all the mentioned works. But if the works were not done in obedience to Him then these workers are calling the wrong person Lord. They were done by "self-will." The worker's own flesh was in charge.

That brings us to the second word—iniquity. Their deception stems from their iniquity, which literally means lawlessness, doing their own thing in the name of Jesus. They have followed after fame and the glory that comes from spectacular miracles. Since pride and self-glorification motivate them, they emulate the Devil's self-willed rebellion. Jesus says "I never knew you." The word "never" in the Greek is "oudepote" which means "not at any time, never at all." These are some of the ministries whose trees produce seed that makes corrupt fruit. They went out on their own rather than stay with established believers , waiting to be discipled.

This is where the third word becomes significant—his Father. The kingdom runs on the will of God, the Father who works through believers for His own glory. Those who enter the kingdom obey Him. These corrupt trees took the power of God's Spirit to perform their ministries and produce their own glory not the Father's.

Simon of Samaria was such a man seeking power and influence over people. The scriptural account is recorded in Acts 8:9:

> But there was a certain man called Simon, who previously practiced sorcery in the city and astonished the people of Samaria, claiming that he was someone great, to whom they all gave heed, from the least to the greatest, saying, "This man is the great power of God." And they heeded him because he had astonished them with his sorceries for a long time. But when they believed Philip as he preached the things concerning the kingdom of God and the name of Jesus Christ, both men and women were baptized. Then Simon himself also believed; and when he was baptized he continued with Philip, and was amazed, seeing the miracles and signs which were done.
>
> Now when the apostles who were at Jerusalem heard that Samaria had received the word of God, they sent Peter and John to them, who, when they had come down, prayed for them that they might receive the Holy Spirit. For as yet He had fallen upon none of them. They had only been baptized in the name of the Lord Jesus. Then they laid hands on them, and they received the Holy Spirit.
>
> And when Simon saw that through the laying on of the apostles' hands the Holy Spirit was given, he offered them money, saying, "Give me this power also, that anyone on whom I lay hands may receive the Holy Spirit."
>
> But Peter said to him, "Your money perish with you, because you thought that the gift of God could be purchased with money! You have neither part nor portion in this matter, for your heart is not right in the sight of God. Repent therefore of this your wickedness, and pray

God if perhaps the thought of your heart may be forgiven you. For I see that you are poisoned by bitterness and bound by iniquity."

Then Simon answered and said, "Pray to the Lord for me, that none of the things which you have spoken may come upon me."

Acts 8:9-24 NKJV

Simon was occupied with power and how it could best serve him. Until Phillip came to town, the people looked to Simon because he had magic power from the evil one. But when Phillip began to minister through the power of the Holy Spirit, the acts of Simon paled into insignificance. He hung around with Phillip trying to learn the secrets of his power. But when he saw the Holy Spirit being given unto the people, he did not ask for the Holy Spirit for himself. No, instead he wanted the position of apostle, to be able to dispense the Holy Spirit. That would have maintained his position above the people. All he wanted was a name and position of power.

Peter read him right. He perceived that he was in the gall of bitterness (because he envied the apostles); and of iniquity (lawlessness), because he wanted the power for his own use. Simon's answer to Peter shows he was still thinking in terms of his sorcery. He knew Peter had pronounced a curse upon him and expected that removing it was in Peter's hands. He utterly failed to understand the nature of the gospel and of God. He was still thinking in the terms of his old god who took every opportunity to carry out a curse.

Legends of Simon Magus, a second century promoter of magic and Gnosticism, are constantly linked with the Simon of Acts because both stood against Christianity by exalting themselves and showing powers of the occult. Both came out of Samaria. Tradition claims that the Simon of Acts left the Church and began a sect of his own, using sorcery and mixing it with tenets of Christianity.

Simon himself was the object of worship in his religion. This was his desire all along. He wanted to be the greatest among men, wielding great power. Is that not what these, whom Jesus denies knowing, are wanting: recognition among men for their great miracles? They are like both Simons: they want the power and the position, but not the Lordship of Jesus.

How does this story relate to the use of power gifts? It shows first that the minister must be under the government of God. That means he first must be a child of the Father. The gifts are just endowments to accomplish the Father's will. They must be worked through the Spirit of God, at Jesus' direction as head, otherwise they are lawless acts. Many a child of the kingdom has lost his gift and his ministry because he failed to do the will of the Father. This is a great loss of joy! Therefore, to maintain our joy in the Lord, we must use His gifts only as the LORD and his Spirit directs. We will not determine whether these men were believers or not, because corrupt teachers can be in either category. Simon, although baptized in water, proves later not to be a true believer. If you recognize corrupt fruit, do not submit to such teaching, believer or not.

How to Stand

This last part of the Law of Understanding actually caps the entire set of laws because producing the fruit of the Spirit the rest of your life is what "standing covers." So, let us look at this portion from that perspective.

> "Therefore whoever hears these sayings of Mine, and does them, I will liken him to a wise man who built his house on the rock: and the rain descended, the floods came, and the winds blew and beat on that house; and it did not fall, for it was founded on the rock.
>
> But everyone who hears these sayings of Mine, and does not do them, will be like a foolish man who built his house on the sand: and the rain descended, the floods came, and the winds blew and beat on that house; and it fell. And great was its fall."
>
> And so it was, when Jesus had ended these sayings, that the people were astonished at His teaching, for He taught them as one having authority, and not as the scribes.
>
> Matthew 7:24-29 NKJV

Again, we have an allegory. The house represents where the man lives spiritually. We are strong or we are weak, according to how we look at life. Anyone can get along in fair weather. It's the storms of life that cause our problems. So the house represents the philosophy of life we have built for ourselves.

The rock is the laws of the kingdom that add stability to our house. If we build our philosophy of life upon these principles, we eliminate self-made problems and have a solid foundation to withstand external problems.

The rain represents our dependency upon God, and by it, He sends blessing or judgment. Water is essential to life. While Adam was in the garden, there was no rain because the rivers and the dew watered it. God had put the management of the garden in Adam's hands. But after man was expelled from the garden, the management of water returned to God's hands. The next mention of rain in the Scriptures came at the time of the flood, when the earth was under judgment. The third mention of rain occurred when Egypt was under judgment (a rain of hail). The fourth mention of rain was for blessing to the farmland. Thus we conclude rain represents the governing of God over our lives. The Law of Impartiality stated that God sends the rain on the just and the unjust, so the government of God falls upon both equally. God sometimes chastens his people with storms. The floods represent overwhelming situations. The waters collect and rise and swirl around the house threatening to overwhelm it and undermine it. But the house built on the rock can take it because the rock resists the power of the temporary flood. Knowledge of what God expects in every situation keeps the house intact.

The sand, on the other hand, shifts with the floods and undermines the underpinnings of the foundation. When a house gets out of square the whole house breaks apart and washes away. Sand is made up of little particles of rock. The problem is not their hardness, but their lack of cohesion and their multitude. If we try to build our lives on any and every philosophy the world has to offer, we are building on sand and our house will not stand.

The wind in Scripture speaks of the force and the power to scatter. In the New Testament, wind sometimes represents various teachings thrust upon the Church by false apostles, called winds of doctrine. These false teachings strike our house in various degrees of force. But the house built on the rock cannot be shaken. When we know God's expectations, other teachings cannot move us.

Conclusion of the Laws

When Jesus finished teaching the people his laws, they were astonished. He didn't debate the issues pro and con as the Rabbis were prone to do. He stated them as absolutes. If you want to be free from bitterness, you must have the right attitude toward your offenses, your sufferings, and your enemies by obeying the laws of Anger, Flexibility, and Impartiality.

If you want to be free from immorality, you must have the right attitude toward your sin, yourself, and others; and obey the laws of Acquisition, Purity, and Criticism.

If you want to be free of temporal values, you must have the right attitude toward God, His Word, and His Kingdom and obey the laws of Devotion, Understanding, and Fidelity.

This is the formula for righteous living! As a result of following this formula, you will develop a likeness to Christ and become like the Father. That amounts to personal holiness and greatly glorifies the Lord. It displays blatant Christianity to the world.

When teaching the Sermon on the Mount Jesus said:

> **Whoever therefore breaks one of the least of these commandments, and teaches men so, shall be called least in the kingdom of heaven; but whoever does and teaches them, he shall be called great in the kingdom of heaven.**
>
> **Matthew 5:19NKJV**

SECTION THREE
Robbers

14

Fruit Robbers

This book would not be complete if it did not include the works and organized efforts of Satan to undo and make of no effect these laws of the kingdom. If he can't keep us from salvation, then his next effort is to rob us of our fruit. There is not a better example of this work than the book of Job. Here God rolls back the curtain of heaven to show how Satan comes against a righteous man.

The first scene in Job opens with a description of the blessings of Job and his faithfulness in being a priest to his family. Then the scene switches to heaven where God confronts Satan with Job's righteousness. What follows is the concentrated campaign against Job by Satan's demonic forces, all with God's permission.

While seeking how to pray for an individual, the Lord gave me a verse in Job. But it made no sense to me, because it pertained to one of the animals in God's discourse with Job at the end of the book. As I pondered what he meant, the Holy Spirit reminded me of an incident in the book The Unseen War by Derek Prince and Don Basham. In it, a man praying to resolve the split in the Church (as a result of the Shepherdship teaching) was shown a wild boar. He told the group that he believed it had something to do with the problem. After they prayed about it, he again saw the boar, but this time it was dead.

Taking my cue from this incident, I looked up "wild boar'" in the concordance. I found it in Psalm 80. The psalmist was bewailing the fact that God had allowed his vineyard (the people of Israel) to have the hedges broken down so that the [wild] boar out of the wood could waste it (Verse 13) and the wild beast out of the field could devour it. I realized from this Scripture that the boar spoken of in The Unseen War and the one in Psalm 80 must have been the same spiritual entity sent to destroy the unity and prosperity of God's people. The wild beasts of the field went after the fruit, while the boar went after the root. Therefore, I concluded that the beasts mentioned in the book of Job were not just random beasts God used in his discourse, but rather the very spiritual beings sent against Job to rob his fruits of righteousness. This discovery led to a detailed study of the beast's natures.

First I noticed that they were all wild except two: the common "behemoth" translated "cattle" all through the Old Testament except here in Job and Leviathan, which was a mythical dragon that equated to Satan himself. The behemoth or water ox, a domestic beast, could easily refer to the flesh while the dragon referred to the Devil. These two beasts were separated from the rest by more dialogue. That left nine to rob the fruits of the Spirit. After all, if Satan cannot induce us to live an evil life all that is left to him is to rob us of the fruit of righteousness and destroy our testimony before the world.

This is what he tried to do to Job. He sent nine powerful wild beast-like spirits to destroy his testimony. Some attempts were successful; others were not. To determine the type of spirits that came after his fruit, we need only look at the animal God chose to represent them and *their ways*.

The Lion

> "Can you hunt the prey for the lion, Or satisfy the appetite of the young lions, When they crouch in their dens,
>
> Or lurk in their lairs to lie in wait?"
>
> **Job 38:39 NKJV**

Lions live in prides made up young and old lions. When there is plenty of food, all enjoy the feeding. However, in hard times, only the fit mature lions are allowed to feed. This preserves the species. The young lions die for lack of food and the old lions live on small game that they are able to catch, otherwise they die also.

The lion, though a powerful beast, is not fast as the herding animals on which he preys. Therefore, to catch his prey he must depend upon waiting in hiding or roaring to instill fear and panic. So, he makes his living off of fear. If the herd animals knew they could outrun him, they probably would not panic and run helter-skelter or in circles; but fear often keeps them from escaping. The Bible has much to say about the lion and his roaring. An angry king is compared to a roaring lion (Prov. 19:12), again causing fear.

When God gave Satan permission to touch Job personally, he used Job's own fear to do it. Job says, "For the thing which I greatly feared is come upon me, and that which I was afraid is come unto me. I was not in safety, neither had I rest, neither was I quiet; yet trouble came" (Job 3:25, 26). I can just see Job after the destruction of his family and possessions thinking, yea worrying, what else can happen that is bad? And then thinking the worst: that horrible disease that Satan thrust upon him.

Job's friends also gave testimony to Job that caused fear (Job 7:14), causing Job to complain that God was hunting him as a fierce lion (Job 10:16). It was not God, but the lion spirit of fear that that stalked him and robbed him of his faith. Job's fear replaced his faith. How else could he say, "I was not in safety, neither had I rest"?

Peter tells us that the devil, like a roaring lion, goes about seeking whom he may devour. Whom may he devour? Those who are afraid! In the presence of faith, he has no power because the Word of God declares him a defeated foe. Therefore, the lion spirit tries to rob us of our faith, and consequently, faithfulness.

The Raven

Who provides food for the raven, When its young ones cry to God, And wander about for lack of food?

Job 38:41 NKJV

The raven, being omnivorous, feeds upon grains, the spoils of fisherman and hunters, eggs, and young defenseless, birds and animals. He is considered to be the most intelligent of all birds. He's very clever and can discern a field of corn just emerging from the ground and pull up the plant to get at the spouting seed, much to the dismay of farmers. He is also a bird that feeds on carrion. He was known in the Bible as one of the birds to clean the battlefield and to pick the eyes from the dead.

From this description, we might say he makes his living the easy, lazy way, by taking from others unable to defend themselves. Though highly intelligent, he seems to be somewhat self-indulgent. Perhaps this is the reason the

Scripture says the young cry unto God for lack. It is not that their parents do not supply their *needs*, it is just that their *wants* greatly exceed their needs. They wander (vacillate or reel or stagger) for lack of meat. In short, they demand more no matter how much is supplied. When we are extremely hungry, we say we are ravenous. I wonder why?

Now, applying this nature to a spirit who is bent on robbing fruit, we could say he promotes poverty through slothfulness, self-indulgence and all manner of desires not backed by diligent labor, or even outright robbery itself, because in essence he is a thief looking for any easy acquisition. He moved upon the Sabians to rob Job of his oxen and asses and the Chaldeans to rob him of his camels. He left Job a pauper. Satan could not attack Job personally because Job was obviously a diligent man.

This robber did not defeat Job, for upon being informed of all his losses he said, "Naked came I out of my mother's womb, and naked shall I return thither: the Lord giveth and the Lord taketh away; blessed be the name of the Lord."

But he will move upon us if we yield to self- indulgence and slothfulness and thus rob us of our self-control or temperance. Proverbs abounds with descriptions of this spirit's work. The sluggard will not plow by reason of the cold, etc. He that loves pleasure, oil and wine shall not be rich (Prov. 21:17). Self indulgence!

The Wild Goat

Knowest thou the time when the wild goats of the rock bring forth? *or* **canst thou mark when the hinds [doe, female deer] do calve?**

> **Canst thou number the months *that* they fulfill? or knowest thou the time when they bring forth?**
>
> **They bow themselves, they bring forth their young ones, they cast out their sorrows.**
>
> **The young ones are in good liking, they grow up with corn; they go forth, and return not unto them.**
>
> **Job 39:1-4 AV**

The whole picture of the wild goats and deer focuses on bearing their young. Evidently, God has created them to have a very difficult birth. Then on top of that, they lose their offspring as soon as they are grown. The whole picture here is pain and loss. It describes a spirit of grief that takes away joy.

This spirit robbed Job of all his joy. He cursed the day he was born. He said, "Oh that my grief were thoroughly weighed (Job 6:2). . . Mine eye also is dim from sorrow (Job 17:7) . . . from crying. He cried for loss of his children, his friends and his position in the community, but most of all for his disillusionment with God. Of course, he did not know that he had become a pawn in the controversy between God and Satan.

The Bible cautions us not to sorrow too much. Paul warned the Corinthians not to inflict "overmuch sorrow" on the disciplined one in 2 Corinthians 2:7-11 lest Satan get an advantage. Evidently, Paul knew about this spirit. He told the Thessalonians, "But I would not have you to be ignorant, brethren, concerning them that are asleep, that ye sorrow not, even as others which have no hope." Again in 2 Corinthians 7:10 he said, "For Godly sorrow worketh repentance to salvation not to be repented of: but the sorrow of the world worketh death," (because of the work of this spirit?)

Several years ago, in an ordinarily routine operation, death struck down the only child of our next-door neighbor. The parents were an older couple who had married late in life and who doted greatly on this child. The spirit of grief took hold of them and within three years both parents were dead also.

Realizing the power grief had in their lives caused me not to grieve overmuch when we lost a twenty-year-old son. I would grieve to a point and then it seemed God would say, "That is enough." I knew he was saved and that thought comforted me. I knew I would see him again.

Jesus has come to defeat this spirit, to comfort all who mourn, (in Isaiah's words) "To appoint them that mourn in Zion, to give them beauty for ashes, the oil of joy for mourning, the garment of praise for the spirit of heaviness" (Isaiah 61:3.) The spirit of grief robs all joy.

The Wild Ass

> **Who hath sent out the wild ass free? or who hath loosed the bands of the wild ass? Whose house I have made the wilderness, and the barren land his dwellings. He scorneth the multitude of the city, neither regardeth he the cry of the driver. The range of mountains is his pasture, and he searcheth after every green thing.**
>
> **Job 39:5-8 AV**

The onager, a native of the Judean desert, is an untamable species of donkey. God has made him to love complete freedom, to do as he pleases, and to wander where he will, free of all restraints including that of a master (crier, shouting orders). He searches on all the mountains for his pleasures (every green thing). His natural habitat is the desert wilderness.

This animal denotes a spirit of rebellion! When a person acts in this manner we call him an "ass." The term originates from the animal's behavior, not his backside, although his backside is the most prominent portion of his anatomy. Perhaps this is why they both came to mean the same thing

Job describes the rebellious (Job 24:5-13) as such when he says, "Behold, as wild asses in the desert they go forth to their work . . . They are those that rebel against the light; they know not the ways thereof, nor abide in the paths thereof." The men Job referred to were victims of this spirit, but there is no indication that Job himself was robbed by it. This spirit robs meekness, and Job exhibited meekness all through his trials. Anger flares when the rebellious cannot have their way. Job was angry with his three friends, but he answered them without violence, remaining fully in control of his temper.

The spirit of the wild ass can rob us of meekness if we can be enticed to rebel. Therefore, we would do well to watch out for this temptation to walk out of the path or to disobey the Lord by living a free independent life in our flesh. A free spirit in the world leads to rebellion. Rebels live in the desert barren of God's blessings. Meekness flourishes under the control of the Master.

The Wild Ox

Will the unicorn be willing to serve thee, or abide by thy crib? Canst thou bind the unicorn with his band in the furrow? or will he harrow the valley's after thee? Wilt thou trust him, because his strength is great? or wilt

thou leave thy labour to him? Wilt thou believe him, that he will bring home thy seed, and gather it into thy barn?

Job 39:9-12 AV

The Biblical unicorn was not the same as the European mythical unicorn, today pictured as a one-horned horse associated with mystical memorabilia. This ancient unicorn had two horns. The Hebrew word for it was "re' em," very close to the Assyrian "rima," which was rendered by their artists to be a very large, wild ox known as the auroch, now extinct. Most Biblical scholars believe this was the animal referred to in Job.

The auroch was an enormous and fierce animal. He was black. He stood six feet tall at the shoulder and he had long double curving horns. Psalm 22 made reference to these horns:

Save me from the lion's mouth: for thou hast heard me from the horns of the unicorns.

Psalm 22:21 AV

Here the horns are equated to the same danger as the lion's mouth. Dangerous! The upper passage indicated the same thing. The questions put to Job were: 1. Can you tame him (get him to live in your barn and bind him in the furrow)? 2. Will he do your will? 3. Will you trust him? 4. Can you leave the labor to him? 5. Will you believe him? If you can't trust him, then why? Because he is extremely dangerous!

Other Bible passages mention his great strength. Balaam blessed Israel by saying, "he hath as it were the strength of a unicorn" (Num. 23:22; 24:8) When Moses blessed Joseph before his death he said, "His glory is like the firstling of his bullock, and his horns are like the horns of unicorns: and with them he shall push the people together to the ends of the earth. . . ." Since his strength and the power of his horns stands out, I think we can conclude that this was a powerful and dangerous beast.

Other bulls in the bos family can have a dangerous temperament as well. A certain wild buffalo in Africa, if angered by a man will hunt him or tree him and wait around three days to take revenge upon him. Other members of the bovine family can become angry beasts, especially dairy bulls. My husband was gored by a Holstein bull we had raised from a calf. He was putting water in a bucket for him and touched his head and told him to move over. Instead, he lunged, lifted up my husband on his horn and tossed him ten away feet to the ground. Fortunately, the horn only penetrated the skin above the rib cage or my husband would have been killed.

This type of animal represents a spirit full of anger seeking revenge. It indulges an unforgiving malice toward those who come against it and carries out Satan's desire for destruction of righteous men. This type of spirit inspires violence and robs the fruit of gentleness. It is because of this spirit that God commands us not to take revenge. "Vengeance is mine saith the Lord, I will repay" (Romans 12:19b). Practicing revenge and holding anger exercises and makes stronger a violent nature, just opposite to the fruit of the Spirit.

Job was provoked by the adversity of his three friends, but in the end God healed him when he forgave them and prayed for them. So the wild ox spirit didn't rob him of his gentleness even though he became exasperated with their accusations.

It will do the same for us. Forgiveness defeats this beast and leads to gentleness in our lives.

The Ostrich

"The wings of the ostrich wave proudly, But are her wings and pinions like the kindly stork's? For she leaves her eggs on the ground, She forgets that a foot may crush them, Or that a wild beast may break them. She treats her young harshly, as though they were not hers; Her labor is in vain, without concern, Because God deprived her of wisdom, And did not endow her with understanding. When she lifts herself on high, She scorns the horse and its rider.

Job 39:13-18 NKJV

The ostrich's whole existence pictures selfishness, carelessness and foolishness. This spirit robs the fruit of love. Contrary to what most people think, the opposite to love is not hatred, but carelessness coupled with selfishness. For this reason God's purest picture of love in the natural world is that of a mother for her child.

He begins by contrasting the ostrich to the stork. The stork, well-known for its parenting prowess, has become a symbol for bringing babies in our society. The ostrich, on the other hand, has beautifully adorned wings that never cover her eggs. Instead, the eggs of several hens are pooled. Perhaps one reason is that they live in small flocks with one male to seven or eight hens. The male sits on them at night and the hens take turns during the day. Since each hen lays several eggs and they are so large, one bird could never cover them. Many of the eggs get broken before they can hatch. This also explains why the female is so indifferent to her own eggs. She doesn't know which ones are her own, thus she labors by habit, not devotion and carefulness. God says that her labor is vain since she has no fear for the eggs being broken. Carelessness!

What a picture of corrupt society's child-raising policies we see in this type! Plato, in presenting his perfect society in *The Republic,* advocated that the state raise the children in nurseries. Hitler tried it in his program to raise up a super race. Certain elements in our society are moving in that direction today. If Satan can destroy the family, then he will eliminate the one place pure love is produced in the world. This type of society would lead to selfish indifference toward the young and mere lust between the parents.

Another characteristic of the ostrich is her utter foolishness. She demonstrates this foolishness by her flight. Although she cannot fly, she uses her wings to lift up her body as she runs. Consequently, running at 40 to 50 miles per hour she can easily outrun a horseman. But because of her foolishness she runs in circles and two or three horsemen can easily catch her. The World Book Encyclopedia states that the ostrich's greatest weakness is her lack of good sense.

Job was attacked by this love-robbing spirit through his own beloved wife. As soon as he was stricken with disease she said to him, "Dost thou still retain thine integrity, curse God and die" (Job 2:9). But Job realized that was not like his wife to speak thus, so he replied, "Thou speakest as one of the foolish women speakest." She probably had this fleeting thought, "He's lost all our possessions and now he's covered with disease, what good is he to me now"? Selfishness.

But even if that was not her thinking, how much compassion and concern for Job were in her words? Actually, they were loaded with a sneer against his faith in God. "Dost thou still retain thine integrity." This is strong evidence that a spirit was influencing her. Had Job not realized that she spoke out of character, their relationship might have been destroyed. But since they later had another family, we know it turned out all right.

Foolishness can destroy households. Proverbs 14:1 says:

Every wise woman buildeth her house: but the foolish plucketh it down with her hands."

How does the wise woman build?

Through wisdom is an house builded; and by understanding it is established. And by knowledge shall the chambers be filled with all precious and pleasant riches.

Proverbs 24:3, 4AV

Contrast this with the foolish woman.

A foolish woman is clamorous: she is simple, and knoweth nothing.

* * *

Stolen waters are sweet, and bread eaten in secret is pleasant. **Proverbs 9:13, 17 AV**

The foolish woman casts her eye upon others and thus destroys the relationship with her husband. She tears down her house. Foolishness, carelessness and selfishness destroy love.

The War Horse

"Have you given the horse strength? Have you clothed his neck with thunder? Can you frighten him like a locust? His majestic snorting strikes terror. He paws in the valley, and rejoices in his strength; He gallops into the clash of arms. He mocks at fear, and is not frightened; Nor does he turn back from the sword. The quiver rattles against him, The glittering spear and javelin. He devours the distance with fierceness and rage; Nor does he come to a halt because the trumpet has sounded. At the blast of the trumpet he says, 'Aha!' He smells the battle from afar,

The thunder of captains and shouting.

Job 39:19-25 NKJV

Man has developed a close association with the horse through the ages. He is intelligent and thus easily trained. He can adapt to all manner of conditions. Because of this adaptability he can live in the wild in most climates, even the desert, but he does best when given a steady diet and shelter from the elements.

Early man soon learned that in warfare the man on horseback had a decided advantage over the man on foot. Thus, the horse became an important factor in warfare. During the crusades, the Europeans rode a broad, lumbering breed of horse into battle. Covered with armor, the horses acted somewhat like a tanks on the battlefield as they bowled over their opponents. The Arabs, however, often out-maneuvered them with their light cavalry of Arabian stock.

In Scripture horses are completely associated with warfare. We read about men or women riding upon asses and plowing with oxen. The only time we read about horses is in connection with chariots and battle. The war horse was bred especially for conflict. The passage in Job is almost poetic in the description of his strength, his fearlessness and his adaptation to the weapons of men. He has been trained to love the battle, and it is obvious he cannot wait to get into it.

The war-horse is a picture of one who loves strife and therefore is prepared to rob peace. Job's peace was continually disturbed by all those who had turned against him. Poor Job, he thought it was God moving against him. He says:

> His troops come together, and raise up their way against me, and encamp around about my tabernacle.
>
> He hath put my brethren far from me, and mine acquaintance are very estranged from me. My kinfolk have failed, and my familiar friends have forgotten me. They that dwell in mine house, and my maids, count me for a stranger: I am alien in their sight. I called my servant, and he gave me no answer; I entreated him with my mouth. My breath is strange to my wife, though I entreated for the children's sake of my own body. Yea, young children despised me; I arose, and they spoke against me. All my inward friends abhorred me: and they whom I loved are turned against me.
>
> **Job 19:12-19AV**

Job's entire familiar world turned against him. Job recognized that it was a warring situation, but not knowing about the Satanic attack, he blamed God.

This spirit is active in stirring up trouble between the ethnic groups of the world today, but it has come against the Church for centuries. He seems to delight in causing conflict between brethren. Several years ago before I knew about this spirit we were praying about a conflict in our church in a home prayer meeting. I mentioned that my husband and I were praying about a conflicted situation when our leader was ministering out of town. We came against the forces of darkness as the cause. Our leader confirmed that the conflict resolved at that moment.

We decided to do the same with the present conflict. After we prayed, a brother suddenly exclaimed, "I just saw a whole herd of horses galloping away. And I believe they were the problem." Now I know what he saw. They were war horses of strife come to rob our unity.

The Hawk

Does the hawk fly by your wisdom, And spread its wings toward the south?

Job 39:26 NKJV

The wisdom of God has made the hawk to fly by wondrous means. Though he flies high, he still has a grand command of what transpires on the ground. The hawk has unique eyesight. His eyes are eight times sharper than man's. With his swift wings he can pounce down on his prey with lightning speed. God armed the hawk with sharp, curving talons for tearing flesh, and their vise-like grip can catch, crush and carry off their prey. Their sharp-hooked beaks enable them to crush bones and then eat all of their victims, including the fur or feathers.

But as ruthless as they are in feeding, they can't stand up to bitter cold weather. Instead, their powerful wings take them south.

God couldn't have chosen a better example of the robber of mercy. This spirit inspires fault-finding. He has a keen eye to seek out flaws. Then he swoops in for the kill with his hooked beak. Nevertheless, turn the tables on him and he can't take it. He'll fly south every time!

Job felt the sharp beak of this spirit through the criticism and accusations of his friends. He even gave them a sharp rebuff himself several times.

> **The young Elihu was angry with the lack of wisdom shown by Job's three friends. Then the wrath of Elihu, the son of Barachel the Buzite, of the family of Ram, was aroused against Job; his wrath was aroused because he justified himself rather than God Also against his three friends his wrath was aroused, because they had found no answer, and yet had condemned Job.**
>
> **Job 32:3 NKJV**

I have often wondered why it is easier to criticize and find fault than it is to praise. Now I believe it must be because we have help from the hawk's eye when we look at our brethren. No wonder then that the Scriptures exhort us to think on true, honest, and lovely things of good report rather than zeroing in on our brothers' faults.

The Eagle

Does the eagle mount up at your command, And make its nest on high? On the rock it dwells and resides, On the crag of the rock and the stronghold. From there it

spies out the prey; Its eyes observe from afar. Its young ones suck up blood; And where the slain are, there it is."

Job 39:27-30 NKJV

The eagle resembles the hawk in many ways, although he is much larger. He is a swift flier and has strong talons and keen eyesight. He also has a curved beak, except it is more pronounced (nearly half the size of his head) with a decided hook. He is especially known for his high, almost effortless flying. And no wonder—since he has a wing span of several feet. Solomon wrote that "the way of an eagle in the air" was one of four wonderful things he had observed.

An eagle builds his nest on the highest crag or tree. It is so large that two wagon loads would hardly carry the sticks. The nest is often seven feet high and six feet across. Truly he is an impressive bird.

Traditionally, the eagle was a symbol of power. Ancient empires used him as their standard. The Romans placed a golden eagle on the tip of a spear and carried it into battle. Each legion marched behind one. The German conquerors used it as their symbol. A double-headed eagle was on the imperial Russian and Austrian coat of arms. A black eagle was the emblem of Prussia. The United States adopted it in 1787. The latest country to take this standard was Hitler's Germany.

The picture here is power. The old adage "power corrupts and absolute power corrupts absolutely" is perhaps the idea God wants to show us. In the Scripture, the eagle is an example of God. As an eagle, God stirs his nest. One of the four living creatures surrounding the throne has the head of an eagle. Since their heads depict the offices of

Christ, the eagle recognizes the supreme power of Christ as Son of God. God is the only one good enough to handle absolute power. Satan himself was corrupted by desiring the power equal to God. Thus, the eagle as a robber of fruit would rob goodness.

Men in high office are often tempted because of their authority. They use their positions to get what they want. For instance, when King David sent for Bathsheba, he knew who she was and to whom she belonged. Yet the Scriptures say he sent messengers and took her. She had no recourse but to come, as the king had commanded it. Then he compounded his sin of adultery with murder by commanding Uriah's death. No doubt the eagle spirit tempted David and ruined his reputation as a good man.

God forgave his sin, but it took a terrible toll on his life. When Nathan confronted David with his sin, he did so by a hypothetical example. David pronounced a curse upon himself by saying the man in the situation should pay back fourfold. Being king, he had the authority to pronounce judgment. Then Nathan said, "Thou art the man." David lost four sons because of his sin. What was worse, he lost his good name.

Other men in powerful positions have fallen prey to this same spirit. Curiously, the powerful seem to fall into sexual sin like David. History is strewn with the scandals of kings and presidents. The escapades of the royal house of Britain filled the tabloids of recent years.

Even Christian leaders have fallen prey to the eagle. The higher they rise in fame and ministry, the more susceptible they become. Satan knows if he can besmirch a leader, the cause of Christ loses stature.

Job had a powerful position in the community. His reputation for goodness reached all the way to heaven. Satan sent the eagle after him but Job resisted. He said,

> "I have made a covenant with my eyes; Why then should I look upon a young woman? For what is the allotment of God from above, And the inheritance of the Almighty from on high? Is it not destruction for the wicked, And disaster for the workers of iniquity? Does He not see my ways, And count all my steps? "If I have walked with falsehood, Or if my foot has hastened to deceit, Let me be weighed on honest scales, That God may know my integrity. If my step has turned from the way, Or my heart walked after my eyes, Or if any spot adheres to my hands Then let me sow, and another eat; Yes, let my harvest be rooted out."If my heart has been enticed by a woman, Or if I have lurked at my neighbor's door, Then let my wife grind for another, And let others bow down over her. For that would be wickedness; Yes, it would be iniquity deserving of judgment.
>
> **Job 31:1-6 NKJV**

Job knew that the eye was the door to lust, so he wouldn't allow what he saw to prey upon his mind. Being pure in God's eyes was more important to him than temporal pleasures. He hated sexual sin and called it a heinous crime to be punished by the judge.

The eagle spirit robs goodness and purity. Satan knows that if our hearts are full of lust either for power or sex, we cannot see God. If we cannot see God, we will not become like Him.

Conclusion

Jesus put forth the laws of righteousness to develop the fruits of the Spirit. Satan counters with Fruit Robbers.

Being aware of what God expects of us by knowing and following his laws, we will thwart the fruit robbers. If we would stand before the judgment seat of Christ full of good fruits, then our lives will also be filled with good works, worthy of reward. Why do I say that? Because fruitful lives translate into kindnesses for others, ministry to others, and obedience to the Lord. Peter sums it up:

> "... As His divine power has given to us all things that pertain to life and godliness, through the knowledge of Him who called us by glory and virtue, by which have been given to us exceedingly great and precious promises, that through these you may be partakers of the divine nature, having escaped the corruption that is in the world through lust.
>
> But also for this very reason, giving all diligence, add to your faith virtue, to virtue knowledge, to knowledge self-control, to self-control perseverance, to perseverance godliness, to godliness brotherly kindness, and to brotherly kindness love. For if these things are yours and abound, you will be neither barren nor unfruitful in the knowledge of our Lord Jesus Christ. For he who lacks these things is shortsighted, even to blindness, and has forgotten that he was cleansed from his old sins.
>
> Therefore, brethren, be even more diligent to make your calling and election sure, for if you do these things you will never stumble; for so an entrance will be supplied to you abundantly into the everlasting kingdom of our Lord and Savior Jesus Christ.
>
> **2 Peter 2-11 NKJV**

SECTION FIVE
Rewarding Works

Rewarding Personal Unworthiness

Many Christians believe erroneously that we shall all be alike when we get to heaven. However, while we have the same type of resurrected body as Jesus, we will only be what we have already become while walking on the earth. So don't think that a magical change at the resurrection will turn you into a super saint. Speaking about the time when God fulfills Revelation, the Bible says:

> "He who is unjust, let him be unjust still; he who is filthy, let him be filthy still; he who is righteous, let him be righteous still; he who is holy, let him be holy still."
>
> **Revelation 22:11 NKJV**

God judges all men according to where they are when their lives end. God, in his grace provided: 1.) Salvation from the consequences of our sin; 2.) The Holy Spirit to live in us and help us change from our selfish nature to God's nature; 3.) The teachings of the Sermon on the Mount, to show us how to live; And 4.) The rest of our lives to learn how to serve under his Lordship.

Paul's advice to the Philippians was to ". . . work out your own salvation with fear and trembling" (Phil. 2:12b). Why did he say "with fear and trembling?" Because works bring consequences, works will be judged. Yes, promised rewards and an inheritance go to the faithful servants who walked in the mode of the Spirit during their lives, but what about the unfaithful servants? Remember, God serves justice at the judgment seat of Christ. Unfaithful servants who frittered away their lives on the pleasures of the flesh in the world, walking on the broad way, not serving the Master, but self, do not inherit the kingdom of God. Yes, they belong in the family of God because God always keeps his word. At some point they accepted Jesus' offer of salvation, but they didn't continue to follow Christ in their walk to the end of their lives.

These Christians miss out on the privileges and pleasures afforded those who walked close to Jesus. These equate to the seed that fell on rocky or thorny ground in the parable of the sower. They didn't produce *any* fruit. Now they must worship him from afar. Neither do they inherit a position for reigning in the Millennial Kingdom. They were not faithful witnesses for Christ, therefore they did not suffer any rejection from the world. Paul told Timothy, "If we suffer, we shall also reign with him: If we deny him, he also will deny us" (2 Timothy 2:12). Deny us what—rewards for faithful service, or a position in his kingdom? These Christians lose rewards at the judgment seat of Christ.

Many lose the significance of the warnings in the New Testament about this loss of rewards because they interpret scriptures referring to them incorrectly. They apply them to mere professing Christians rather than genuine believers. One reason is the word "perdition," as it is used in today's language. Even Webster's New World Dictionary defines "perdition" as coming from a Latin word *perdere* –

to lose. But then defines it theologically as "loss of the soul—hell." This is pure interpretation. The Greek word used in the scripture also speaks of loss, but falls short of *always* speaking of the soul's eternal state. Sometimes it is applied to believers, not meaning loss of salvation, but loss of rewards. According to Strong's Expanded Exhaustive Concordance[6] "perdition" comes from the word *apoleia* which means "loss of well being, not loss of being, used of things signifying their waste or ruin." This word itself is derived from another Greek word *appalumi*, which means-- a. to destroy utterly b. the idea is not extinction, but ruin, loss--not of being, but well being. This same Greek word is translated "destruction" in Philippians 3:18c, 19, "of enemies of the cross[7] . . . whose end is *apoleia (ruin)* . . . who mind earthly things. Also 2 Peter 3:16, 17 where he condemns ignorant teachers to the category of losers.

> ". . . which they that are unlearned and unstable wrest [Paul's teaching] as they do other scriptures, to their own *apoleia (loss or ruin)* Ye therefore, beloved, seeing ye know these things before, beware lest ye also, being led away with the error of the wicked, fall from your own steadfastness.

Teachers who wrongly divide the scriptures can be ashamed at the judgment seat of Christ (2 Timothy 2:15). God is jealous for his Word because it is the source of our spiritual growth.

For this reason James warned, "My brethren, let not many of you become teachers, knowing that we shall re-

---

[6] A New addition (2001) put out by Thomas Nelson Publishers, which includes Vine's Dictionaries, word studies from Brown-Driver-Briggs Hebrew and English Lexicon, Baur-Arndt-Gingrich-Danker and Theological Wordbook of the Old Testament

[7] Jesus said, "Take up thy cross and follow me." These Christians were not using their cross to put the flesh to death.

ceive a stricter judgment." (3:1 NKJV). Jesus came down hard on the Pharisees because they taught Israel leading them astray.

Since all spiritual growth of the new believer depends upon understanding of the Bible, he must have teachers to teach him certain basic truths of his new life. If the teaching does not come from the Holy Spirit, or is twisted, his walk will become flawed at its beginning.

False teaching does damage to the Church. Whole denominations have been built on teaching that curbs their growth to maturity. Therefore, besides those who ignore God's claims on their life by living in the flesh or in the world, God denies teachers the kingdom of God when they persist in their perversion of truth.

Paul warned the builders of God's building (the Church) to take heed how they built. He said:

> **Now he who plants and he who waters are one, and each one will receive his own reward according to his own labor. For we are God's fellow workers; you are God's field, you are God's building. According to the grace of God which was given to me, as a wise master builder I have laid the foundation, and another builds on it. But let each one take heed** *how he builds on it.* **For no other foundation can anyone lay than that which is laid, which is Jesus Christ. Now if anyone builds on this foundation with gold, silver, precious stones, wood, hay, straw, each one's work will become clear; for the Day will declare it, because it will be revealed by fire; and the fire will test each one's work, of what sort it is. If anyone's work which he has built on it endures, he will receive a reward. If anyone's work is burned, he will suffer loss; but he himself will be saved, yet so as through fire. Do you not know that you are the temple**

of God and that the Spirit of God dwells in you? If anyone *defiles* the temple of God, God will *destroy* him. For the temple of God is holy, which temple you are.

1 Corinthians. 3:8-17 NKJV

Here Paul is talking to the Corinthian Church corporately, the whole Church is the temple of God. Therefore, when he talks of any minister that defiles the temple, he says God will defile him. tit for tat, like for like, because the words defile and destroy are the same word in the Greek just translated differently here.

Paul even warned Timothy, his own son in the faith, of the necessity of careful study:

Study to show thyself approved unto God, a workman *that needeth not to be ashamed*, **rightly dividing the word of truth.**

2 Timothy 2:15 AV (Emphasis added)

Many people desire to be teachers to gain importance in the church. God gives gift and calls his real teachers, others presume to teach, using the precepts of men. Presumptuous "truth" has damaged whole denominations, causing their adherents loss of rewards. Like the corrupt fruit from corrupt ministries, corrupt teaching distorts truth. God judges teachers more severely than others. Even if some teachers have entered the kingdom, they could be ashamed before him if they don't divide the Scriptures correctly.

False prophets add another category to losers at the judgment seat of Christ. Remember them as taking away joy in the last law of the kingdom in the Sermon on the Mount? Let's look at this passage again from the perspective of believers being deceived by their own pride.

> Even so, every good tree bears good fruit, but a bad tree bears bad fruit. A good tree cannot bear bad fruit, nor can a bad tree bear good fruit. Every tree that does not bear good fruit is cut down and thrown into the fire. Therefore by their fruits you will know them. "Not everyone who says to Me, 'Lord, Lord,' shall enter the kingdom of heaven, but he who does the will of My Father in heaven. Many will say to Me in that day, 'Lord, Lord, have we not prophesied in Your name, cast out demons in Your name, and done many wonders in Your name?' And then I will declare to them, 'I never knew you; depart from Me, you who practice lawlessness!'
>
> **Matthew 7:21-23 NKJV**

This passage of Scripture is controversial. So we must look at it carefully to realize what it actually says. Remember when we examined it in the "joy robbers" column? We talked about the tree coming from a seed, not a slip of the original tree. We can never depend on a seed of a fruit tree producing the same as the mother tree.

Notice in the passage above that it is the tree, which represents his ministry that is thrown into the fire, not the worker. Can a true believer be considered a ravening wolf? Does this not speak of an unbeliever masquerading as a Christian? Probably. But can it not also apply to men trying to build the Church their own way, destroying believers under their teaching?

One of the building materials was wood, which would be burned. Is this not work whose fruit was unacceptable, whether it be a vine that only produced leaves or a fruit tree that produced sour fruit? Both are made of wood. This is the highest form of building material in the flesh: works that can't pass through the judgment fire

Add to that thought what Jesus said that "Not everyone who called him Lord, would enter the kingdom of heaven." These men worked rebellion. They never took the time to know the Father's plan; they had their own. For this reason Jesus said, "I never, ever knew you. He was the administrative head of the body of Christ. If they had listened to him, they would have acted in response to His will, building up the Church.

Instead, they built their own ministries, fleecing the sheep to do it. Actually, many of these men gave the Church a bad name before the world, begging money in flashy TV campaigns while their personal lives lacked the traits of God. Even though some of the miracles performed were genuine because the Holy Spirit ministers to the needs of his people. Jesus denies the workers any reward. They got the glory for the miracles, not God. They had their reward on earth.

Paul speaks of the judgment seat of Christ as a fearful event. He maintains that our labor for Christ has to be "acceptable" (2 Corinthians. 5:9). He further says it will be judged at the judgment seat of Christ as "good or *bad*." "Knowing the terror of the Lord, we persuade men; but we are made manifest . . ." says Paul concerning his labor—in contrast to the false teaching of the Judaizers who opposed him. They will face a stern Jesus at the judgment seat for their destruction in the early church.

Another example of false teachers, etc. losing rewards is those subtracting truth from God's plans for the future in the book of Revelation.

And if anyone cancels *or* takes away from the statements of the book of this prophecy—these predictions relating to Christ's kingdom and its speedy triumph, to-

> gether with the consolations and admonitions (warnings) pertaining to them—God will cancel *and* take away from him his share in the tree of life and in the city of holiness (pure and hallowed) which are described *and* promised in this book.
>
> **Revelation 22:19 AMP**

These had a part reserved for them that they could not claim. They lost their part in the tree of life and their part in the city (New Jerusalem). Contrast this loss with those blessed saints who enjoy these privileges.

> Blessed are they that wash their robes [by keeping his commandments], that they may have the right to come to the tree of life, and may enter in by the gates into the city.
>
> **Revelation 22:14 ASV**

The losers cannot partake of the tree of life or enter the city through the gates. This does not mean some are not saved. Instead, these deceived ones are those who deceived themselves by the liberalism served in seminaries on earth. The deceiving teachers are those who taught men zealous to serve as pastors the precepts of men, spoiling their future ministry to the Church. As disobedient children, God puts them in "timeout." He doesn't condemn them to hell like unbelievers, but gives them a just reward for their worthlessness to Christ, in a place, where there shall be "weeping and gnashing of teeth." The weeping shows their regrets. After being "somebody" among men, they end up being a "nobody" just outside the blessed city.

Who else will join them in this place? Look at the verse following the blessed in heaven:

> [But] without are the dogs and those who practice sorceries (magic arts) and impurity [the lewd, adulterers] and the murderers and idolaters and everyone who loves and deals in falsehood (untruth, error, deception, cheating).
>
> Revelation 22:15 AMP

Whoa, how can these be Christians? Wait! Compare these Scriptures.

> **Know ye not that the unrighteous shall not inherit the kingdom of God? Be not deceived: neither fornicators, or idolaters, nor adulterers, nor effeminate, nor abusers of themselves with mankind,**
>
> **Nor thieves, nor covetous, nor drunkards, nor revilers, nor extortioners, shall inherit the kingdom of God.**
>
> **And such were some of you: but ye are washed, but ye are sanctified, but ye are justified in the name of the Lord Jesus, and by the Spirit of our God.**
>
> 1 Corinthians. 6:9-11 AV

Paul goes on to say he will not allow himself to be brought under the power of any [thing] that diverts him from serving God. Then he explains, "Be followers of me." From the tone of this chapter it appears that some of these believers had slipped back into their old lifestyle. They were going to court against each other, probably for some of the offenses mentioned above. Paul warns that such behavior does not inherit the kingdom of God. How can this be talking about unbelievers when they have *no chance* of inheriting? Paul tells them flatly that he who does these things does not inherit!

Now compare another like Scripture:

> Now the works of the flesh are evident, which are: adultery, fornication, uncleanness, lewdness idolatry, sorcery, hatred, contentions, jealousies, outbursts of wrath, selfish ambitions, dissensions, heresies, envy, murders, drunkenness, revelries, and the like; of which I tell you beforehand, just as I also told you in time past, that *those who practice such things will not inherit the kingdom of God.*

Galatians 5:19-21 NKJV (Emphasis added)

They that do such things shall not inherit! Paul wrote both of these passages to Christians warning them to avoid walking in the flesh. That opens the possibility that some will not heed the warning. Now compare these lists with the works mentioned in Revelation 22:15AV: "For without are dogs, and sorcerers, and whoremongers, and murderers, and idolaters, and whosoever loveth and maketh a lie.

But first let's answer the question, "Without where? Without the city " These without the city have the same sins as those who do not inherit. Looking at the Online Bible for meanings of the word in each category we find this:

Dog = kuon – a dog, as a metaphor – a man of impure mind. Does this not equate to adultery, fornication, and lasciviousness? Jude says these characterize the end-time church, where some are believers (Jude 19-23).

Sorcerer – pharmakos – Pertaining to magical arts--witchcraft?

Whoremonger - Pornos - 1. A man who prostitutes his body to another man for hire. 2. A male prostitute. 3. A man who indulges in unlawful sexual intercourse and fornication? A child molester?

Murderer – a homicide Also a crime against a nation such as assassination

Idolater – worshippers of false gods used of Christians participating in any worship of the heathen especially of one who attends their sacrificial feasts and eats the remains of offered victims.

Loves –to love, do like, or sanction . . . and loves the lie

Lie – pseudo – a. a lie, b. a conscious and deliberate falsehood, c. in a broad sense whatever is not what it seems to be (a hypocrite?), d. of perverse, impious, deceitful precepts—Teachers of error? Loving all these?

Are not these same sins mentioned in the works of the flesh, which Paul declared would disinherit saints? Do Christians do these things today? What about the Catholic priests who molested little boys? What about homosexuality in the Church, even among pastors? What about the addictions to pornography among the men of the Church? What about teachers of erroneous new heresies prophesied for the end-time Church—liars?

The perpetrators of these sins have not washed their robes. They remain spotted by the flesh. Revelation 22:15 places them outside the city, but where?

Jesus tells of a place where believers in God will be cast into an outer darkness

> The centurion answered and said, "Lord, I am not worthy that You should come under my roof. But only speak a word, and my servant will be healed. For I also am a man under authority, having soldiers under me. And I say to this one, 'Go,' and he goes; and to another, 'Come,' and he comes; and to my servant, 'Do this,' and he does it." When Jesus heard it, He marveled, and said to those who followed, "Assuredly, I say to you, I have not found such great faith, not even in Israel. And I say

> to you that many will come from east and west, and sit down with Abraham, Isaac, and Jacob in the kingdom of heaven. But the *sons of the kingdom will be cast out into outer darkness.* There will be weeping and gnashing of teeth." Then Jesus said to the centurion, "Go your way; and as you have believed, so let it be done for you." And his servant was healed that same hour.
>
> **Matthew 8:8-13 NKJV (Emphasis added)**

Many of the Jews, who believe in and worship the true God still await their promises to be fulfilled, but are still blinded to the gospel. Are they counted the children of the kingdom in Jesus' eyes? One cannot help but wonder if Jews faithful to God through these two thousand years will also be sent to the outer darkness in a heavenly ghetto after their resurrection because they remained true to God as they knew him, but they rejected Jesus, their Messiah, in their lifetime.

Then concerning the Church, in Matthew 22:13 Jesus tells the parable of the guest at the Wedding feast without a wedding garment.

> But when the king came in to see the guests, he saw a man there who did not have on a wedding garment. So he said to him, 'Friend, how did you come in here without a wedding garment?' And he was speechless. Then the king said to the servants, 'Bind him hand and foot, *take him away, and cast him into outer darkness;* there will be weeping and gnashing of teeth. For many are called, but few are chosen.
>
> **Matthew 22:13, 14 NKJV (Emphasis added)**

Why was he rejected? Did he presume to participate in the wedding festivities in an unwashed garment, still spotted by the flesh? Look at Revelation 19:7-9a: AV

> **Let us be glad and rejoice and give Him glory, for the marriage of the Lamb has come, and** *His wife has made herself ready."* **And to her it was granted to be arrayed in fine linen, clean and bright, for the fine linen is the righteous acts of the saints. Then he said to me, "Write: 'Blessed are those who are called to the marriage supper of the Lamb!'"** (Emphasis added)

Apparently, of those called, the "ready" were chosen.

In the parable of the talents, Matthew 25:30 the master dealt the lazy and worthless servant the same blow as the disqualified wedding guest:

> "But his lord answered and said to him, 'You wicked and lazy servant, you knew that I reap where I have not sown, and gather where I have not scattered seed. So you ought to have deposited my money with the bankers, and at my coming I would have received back my own with interest. Therefore take the talent from him, and give it to him who has ten talents.
>
> 'For to everyone who has, more will be given, and he will have abundance; but from him who does not have, *even what he has will be taken away.* And cast the unprofitable servant into the outer darkness. There will be weeping and gnashing of teeth.
>
> Matthew 25:29, 30 NKJV (Emphasis added)

The worthless servant had something, which he held to be more important than that which the master gave him, hence the phrase—take away even that which he hath? some false teaching perhaps? Of course when the Master reveals the full truth, anything false will be taken away. One more example—look what happens to the unfaithful pastor.

> "Who then is a faithful and wise servant, whom his master made ruler over his household, to give them food in due season? Blessed is that servant whom his master, when he comes, will find so doing. Assuredly, I say to you that he will make him ruler over all his goods. But if that evil servant says in his heart, 'My master is delaying his coming,' and begins to beat his fellow servants, and to eat and drink with the drunkards, the master of that servant will come on a day when he is not looking for him and *at an hour that he is not aware of, and will cut him in two and* appoint him his portion with the hypocrites. There shall be weeping and gnashing of teeth.
>
> **Matthew 24:45-51NKJV (Emphasis added)**

Jesus states that this latter man is a ruling servant over the household; therefore we would interpret him to be a pastor or overseer in Christ's Church, Jesus being his Lord. In contrast to the faithful and wise servant, the unfaithful servant's behavior disqualifies him for promotion. Jesus does not mention the outer darkness here, but he does speak of the weeping and gnashing of teeth, which also designates hell. However, the subject being examined here is faithfulness and obedience in works, not a saved or lost position. Pastors who are unsaved are never qualified for promotion or any reward at all, except hell.

In the Law governing the maintenance of Joy, Jesus exhorts his disciples to "Enter into the strait gate," because this narrow way to walk leads to life, and few there be that find it. Here again we have reference to the few who are chosen in contrast to the many who are called. Those that find the strait gate have to see it. Surely those that find His "abundant life" are they that allow the "water of the Word" and the leading of the Spirit to restrict their lives by yielding their bodies as a living sacrifice. Paul says this is a reasonable service for receiving salvation (Romans 12:1). The flamboyant lifestyle of those on the "broad way" keeps them from entering the kingdom. This suggests that not all of those born into the family of God enter into the kingdom of God.

Many of the teachings concerning whether one can lose salvation by our works after we have been born again, come from misunderstanding that we can fail to enter his kingdom by falling back into the flesh. It is not eternal life that they lose, but rights and privileges in the kingdom. Instead, they go merrily along the "broad way," or seeking after the things of this world, wasting their new life purchased by Christ's death.

Why should these believers be rewarded with the same blessings as those who have been obedient to the end of their lives? Even worse, why should false teachers or false prophets enjoy the privileges of the faithful servants? Those who used God's name and power to promote themselves and their fortunes will face a stern-faced Jesus. 1 John 2:4 says: He that saith, I know him, and keepeth not his commandments, is a liar, and the truth is not in him." No wonder Jesus says to them, "I never knew you." The word for "know" here means "to know completely" Mary used the same word when she questioned the angel Gabriel about how she could become pregnant since she "knew" not a man.

These failed to know the Father or the Son. They deserve to be put out of his intimate presence. The writer to the Hebrews says, "The Lord shall judge his people. It is a fearful thing to fall into the hands of the living God (Heb. 10:30b, 31).

Where is this outer darkness of the saved? Some have suggested that it is some far off place, perhaps in outer space. How can these be children of God and not live where the family live?

Look again at Revelation 22:14 AV:

> **Blessed are they that do his commandments, that they** *may have right* **to the tree of life, and may enter in** *through* **the gates into the city. (Emphasis added)**

Remember the teachers who subtracted from the Book of Revelation. They lost their rights to the tree and the city that the blessed gained. Herein lays the answer to a great mystery. Why is the wall to the Heavenly Jerusalem so thick and high, and why does the gate require an angelic guard when they remain open continually?

> **Its gates shall not be shut at all by day (there shall be no night there). And they shall bring the glory and the honor of the nations into it. But there shall by no means enter it anything that defiles, or causes an abomination or a lie, but only those who are written in the Lamb's Book of Life.**
>
> **Revelation 21:25- 27 NKJV**

Those condemned to the outer darkness never repented of their unworthiness before Jesus caught them away to the judgment. Now they reflect on their losses. Notice those who may not enter summarize those outside: they that work abominations and work lies, both defile.

Perhaps God, in his mercy, will release them from their prison in due time, after all, since only believers could be on the premises, their names have to be written in the Lamb's book of life. They have escaped hell and they do have eternal life, a prerequisite for entering the city. They are saved as by fire; losing everything except their eternal life. However, they shall not mingle with the blessed, at least not for now.

I suggest the wall surrounding the city will be their prison. Are the entrances to the wall through the side walls of the gates? Does the guard prevent exit from the wall?

Look at its dimensions! It stands 144 cubits high and 144 cubits broad. We know the length of the wall because it matches the sides of the city, which are 12,000 furlongs, or 1500 miles long per side. By using the great cubit of approximately 21 to 22 inches,[8] the wall measures 264 feet high and broad, and 6,000 miles long in U S linear measurements.

Twenty-two story buildings

If we allowed 12 feet high to a story, the wall would equal a 22 story building in height, while the gate through the wall into the city would be 88 yards deep, just 12 yards shy of a football playing field. That's quite a prison!

---

[8] The Scriptures say (Ezekiel 40:5) the building cubit for Ezekiel's temple is a long cubit, the regular cubit plus a hand span. The hand span is measured at the base of the fingers. In most men that measures four inches. I used the 22 inch measurement for a cubit.

As to it being called the outer darkness, Jesus used the Greek words "exoteros" and "skotos." Exoteros simply means "outer" while "skotos" can mean the darkness of night, but comes from a base word meaning shadow from the interception of light. This combination, "outer darkness" occurs only three times in Scripture, the three times we cited that were spoken by Jesus himself.

In each incident, the people involved expected to be included in God's company. They were all his people. They believed in God, but they failed to live up to "a reasonable service" (Romans 12:1), which caused their rejection. The children of the kingdom, the Jews who held the promise of a great kingdom, refused to recognize their king when he came, and ever since. The Christians refused to take Jesus' commandments seriously, or used His power for their own glorification. Or, like the unfaithful pastor saw Jesus' coming in the far distant future. He was not watching and fell back into the flesh.

As to the outer darkness the differential brightness between the light in the city and the light in the wall makes it a darkened place by comparison. Light in the city shines unhindered because of the clarity of the city structure. One time John refers to it as "clear as crystal" and twice he refers to the gold of it as being "clear as glass." The wall, on the other hand, does not have this clarity. Jasper, generally an opaque stone with a wide variety of colors included, appears in its most precious form as barely translucent.

Why John likened the city to a jasper stone most precious, clear as crystal, we cannot tell. George Fredrick Kunz, once America's foremost gemologist, assigns a green hue to precious jasper.[9] But testimony of Marvin Ford, who glimpsed the city during a clinical death experience in 1972, described the wall as being veined, typical of the jasper as we know it today. He said, "I viewed its walls of jasper consisting of a heavenly green unlike anything I had ever seen before. I could see the marble-like vein running all through it."[10] That's not clear as crystal! Thus, the light he saw shining through it would have been translucent—low light compared to the city whose light shone with the glory of the Lamb!

Conclusion

Saints of God, beware lest you fail to please the LORD. Many of the Church today do not possess a healthy fear of our awesome God. No wonder Paul mentions the "terror" of the Lord that Christians will face at the Judgment seat of Christ. Let us all strive to finish the race with confidence and enjoy an abundant entrance into the kingdom of God! Paul's words to the Colossian Christians make a good final warning:

> **And whatsoever ye do, do it heartily, as unto the Lord. And not unto men; knowing that of the Lord you shall receive the reward of the inheritance: for ye serve the Lord Christ. But** *he that doeth wrong shall receive for the wrong which he hath done:* **and there is no respect of persons.**
>
> **Colossians 3:23-25 (AV Emphasis added)**

---

[9] George Fredrick Kunz, The Curios Lore of Precious Stones (New York: Dover Publications, 1971), p. 90

[10] [10] Anne Sandberg, Seeing the Invisible, Logos International, Plainfield, NJ, 1977 p. 65

16

Rewarding Personal Righteousness

As I mentioned in the first chapter, when Christians stand before the judgment seat of Christ, the only thing being judged is their life in Christ. The life spent living in the flesh before salvation will be discarded. However, if these same sins characterize their lives as believers, evil in their lives has consequences. This is not to say that we all shall not experience a measure of shame for the life that we have wasted in the flesh and suffer a denial of good things in the kingdom. John gave another reason we could be ashamed at the judgment seat of Christ:

> **And now, little children, abide in him; that, when he shall appear, we may have confidence, and not be ashamed before him at his coming.**
>
> **1 John 2:28 AV**

We continue to abide in Christ we will have confidence! The portions of life spent living in the Spirit will be acknowledged and commended. The purpose of this judgment is to reward saints for their faithfulness and to supply a righteous government for the Kingdom Age on earth. The Scripture mentions two different kinds of rewards, and these are further divided into other categories. The first kind of reward mentioned are crowns. These are like badges of honor, similar to the boy-scout badges. There are several of these that are available to each believer. Three crowns are available for overcoming the flesh and two for righteous service.

Crowns for Overcoming The Flesh

In the chapter on the soul we described the flesh as fulfilling the love for the world. We diagrammed it thus:

```
Lust of the Flesh--------------I Feel (Good)----------------------------my Body
Lust of the Eyes---------------I want (money, things, people)----------Will
Pride of Life--------------------I Am (Someone Important)---------------Mind
```

A crown is given for overcoming each of these temptations of the Soul.

The Incorruptible Crown

The crown given for overcoming the lust of the flesh is an incorruptible one. Paul compares winning this crown to winning a laurel wreath in the Greek Olympic games.

> **Do you not know that those who run in a race all run, but one receives the prize? Run in such a way that you may obtain it. And everyone who competes for the prize is temperate in all things. Now they do it to obtain a perishable crown, but we for an imperishable crown.**
>
> 1 Corinthians 9:24-26 NKJV

Paul compares living the Christian life to preparing for the Olympics. An athlete has his eye on one thing: winning the prize for the best. His whole life focuses on that one thing until he runs the race or fights the fight. After the race he returns to a less rigorous life style. Not so with the

Christian race. It runs for the entire lifetime. Moreover, Christians do not compete with one another for the prize. Instead, the Christian runs the race against time. He has an individual racecourse strewn with character building hurdles geared to his particular temperament, strengths and weaknesses. Nevertheless, just as the athlete must keep his focus on the condition of his body for the race, so must a Christian. Paul specifically mentions the problems with the body.

> **Therefore I run thus: not with uncertainty. Thus I fight: not as one who beats the air. But I discipline my body and bring it into subjection, lest, when I have preached to others, I myself should become disqualified.**
>
> **1 Corinthians 9:26, 27 NKJV**

Paul knew the power of the flesh. He knew that to indulge in body lusts could destroy his ministry and deny him the prize. In the next chapter he defined the very fleshly lusts that destroyed Israel in the wilderness. He mentions four things to which the Israelites succumbed: idolatry, fornication, tempting God and murmuring. These same works are mentioned in the list in Galatians 5 as works of the flesh. Paul adds: "of the which I tell you before, as I have also told you in time past, that they which do such things shall not inherit the kingdom of God" (Gal 5:21b).

Believers who allow fleshly desires to hinder their race will not finish the course, and therefore will not receive the full reward. Paul's answer to the problem of the lust of the flesh was to keep the body under control. He that strives for the mastery is temperate in all things. The flesh likes to feel good. If its desires are not curbed, they lead to excesses that control the body. Appetites of the flesh include food, drink, drugs and sex.

Excesses of these desires become characteristic of the evil last days: They shall be eating and drinking and marrying wives (someone else's). Food becomes a big hurdle for some Christians. The taste and smell senses of the body need control or they will clamor for satisfaction. The sight sense aids desire when delectable treats are set before them. When one succumbs to the lust of the flesh he adds excess weight to his body slowing his health and hindering his capacity to function.

Overeating makes the body sluggish and induces sleep and an indolent attitude. The flesh does not desire to exercise, as that would remedy the situation and revive the body. One must exercise a strong will to inaugurate it. Paul told Timothy "that bodily exercise profiteth a little." Although exercise is the remedy for over-eating, even this action can be carried to extreme and given more prominence than prudent. One obsessed with the shape and condition of his body for appearance's sake can go overboard with exercise or dieting. Unhealthy dieting upsets the body and can destroy health as well.

These extreme measures also excite the pride of life to fulfill the lust of the flesh. The secret of success lies in temperance, not excesses of either kind.

Drink and drugs can become a problem when they get control of the flesh. The body becomes addicted and clamors for satisfaction. Drugs and alcohol work on the nervous system and induce good feelings. Yet both alcohol and some drugs have their purpose in creation. The Bible does not teach abstinence in regard to alcohol, but rather temperance.

Sex becomes a problem when its appetites take over the mind. I recently read of a man and a woman whose lives had been ruined by an addiction to sex. Their minds were never free from thinking about their next sexual encounter. Their abnormality cost them their own families and friendships, because the mouth speaks of what is in the heart. Such perversions are demon-inspired bondages.

Child molestation, homosexuality, and lesbianism also fall into this category. According to an interview, some homosexuals have sex eight or nine times a day. This is a terrible bondage to the lust of the flesh. Such excesses lead to heinous crimes against others, particularly children.

God ordained sex as a means of procreation. It is meant to be a joyous union between two individuals committed to each other for life, not an excuse to feed bodily appetites with anybody at anytime in any way. Overcoming the flesh for a lifetime earns a crown of incorruption. Paul was afraid that after having preached to others he might nullify his preaching by giving in to the flesh, therefore he kept his body under strict control. Others we could all name have forfeited this crown by giving in to the appetites of the flesh in sex and ruined their ministries. Temperance and goodness derived by purity are the fruits that earn this crown.

The Crown of Life

The crown of life is awarded to those who overcome two temptations: giving in to the lust of the eyes and clinging to life in this world when confronted with the choice of death or denying Christ.

Jesus said to those faced with martyrdom, "Be faithful until death, and I will give you the crown of life" (Revelation. 2:10 NKJV).

Both these temptations are aimed at seeking temporal desires rather than eternal rewards. Therefore, they test faith. First, let us look at the lust of the eyes.

> **Blessed is the man who endures temptation; for when he has been approved, he will receive the crown of life which the Lord has promised to those who love Him. Let no one say when he is tempted, "I am tempted by God"; for God cannot be tempted by evil, nor does He Himself tempt anyone. But each one is tempted when he is drawn away by his own desires and enticed. Then, when desire has conceived, it gives birth to sin; and sin, when it is full-grown, brings forth death.**
>
> **Do not be deceived, my beloved brethren. Every good gift and every perfect gift is from above, and comes down from the Father of lights, with whom there is no variation or shadow of turning.**
>
> **James 1:12-17 NKJV**

Temptation begins with lust. We are drawn away by desires for temporal things. Demons are always on hand to entice us to go after the object of our desires. We want things that promote our comfort, such as houses, furnishings, cars—especially the expensive or prestigious. Or we want playthings that amuse us and pass our time. We also want attractive and expensive clothing to adorn our persons and lift up our ego.

Yes, and we even want people. Barren women who want children can be so sick with want, that they steal someone else's baby. Lonely or seductive people want other people's spouses. Companies steal away employees from other companies. In the world, people constantly pursue their wants. Excessive wants excite the eyes to the point of covetousness.

The New Testament describes covetousness as a form of idolatry. No wonder, since the object desired becomes the focus of the life instead of God. If we would do as the Scripture says, to let God be the giver of gifts, trusting him who always sees the situation, we would receive all the good things of life. The peace that comes from trusting God's wisdom in his gifts is called contentment. My friend Harry Robinson's definition of happiness is—"liking what you already have." God has promised to give us the desires of our heart if we delight in Him. When we delight in Him, we only desire the good things.

I have experienced this fulfillment many times in my life. It appears I have only to express a desire for something, and the next thing I know it just seems to come to me. I don't have to dwell on the desire. Countless things in my possession just suddenly showed up in various circumstances: most were bargains, some were gifts. A prime example is my computer (not one of the bargains). Several years ago I wanted a computer to make my writing easier. My husband spent about $1500 on a popular set that suited my needs at the time. But as my needs expanded beyond the capabilities of that set, I became frustrated.

As computers grew more powerful, so did the peripheral machines such as laser printers, scanners, modems, and CD players. My computer would not support the new attachments. The value of my machine was now worthless, so it could not be traded in on a new one. Since my husband was not into computers at all, I knew there was no way I could persuade him to put out more money for another system. So I determined to do what I could with the old one and be content.

To my surprise, two of my sons, who were computer buffs themselves, talked him into getting me a set beyond all my desires (and with capabilities I will never need to exceed or so I thought at the time). God moved on his heart, and through my husband's love for me, God's love was expressed and his word fulfilled concerning the desires of my heart.

We often say, "If I only had _____, I would be happy." But that is not true. No sooner than we are in possession of that one thing, our eyes are on something else. Ask this question to anyone you meet no matter how wealthy. "Do you know how much money it will take to make you happy?" You will receive the same reply. "Just a little bit more." The victory over this first part of the temptation lies in being content with the gifts God gives and trusting Him to meet your needs in this temporal sphere.

As I said earlier, the second area of temptation comes as a result of persecution.

> **Do not fear any of those things which you are about to suffer. Indeed, the devil is about to throw some of you into prison, that you may be tested, and you will have tribulation ten days. Be faithful until death, and I will give you the crown of life.**
>
> **Revelation 2:10 NKJV**

If the devil cannot distract you with enticement to things to keep you from being faithful, then he may try to destroy your faith by persecution. After having taken away all of Job's possessions, the devil then attacked his life. Even so Job refused to deny God.

Many a Christian has been faced with the choice of remaining alive in this temporal world or dying a martyr's death.

During the Roman persecution Christians were given this choice: renounce Christ or die. It shows a lack of faith to cling to physical life when He promises eternal spiritual life. Again, Jim Elliot's famous quote says it all: "A man is no fool to give up what he cannot keep in order to gain what he cannot lose."

Jesus exhorted the people whom to fear:

> "And I say to you, My friends, do not be afraid of those who kill the body, and after that have no more that they can do. But I will show you whom you should fear: Fear Him who, after He has killed, has power to cast into hell; yes, I say to you, fear Him!"
>
> Luke 12:4, 5 NKJV

Of course, Jesus was talking about God, the judge. We shall all die eventually. How much better it is to trust our life to God. Jesus said being faithful unto death earns the Crown of Life. It makes no difference if the life is cut short by martyrdom or lived long and full of temptation; remaining faithful is what matters. The temptations of life are merely distractions from obedience. Getting our eyes off Jesus and on temporal things or this temporal life will cost us the Crown of Life.

The Crown of Righteousness

We earn the crown of righteousness for consistent righteous living: staying on course and finishing the race. The alternative would be to leave the track to pursue personal ambitions that promote the ego. This crown is reserved for those believers who do not allow anything in life to become more important than finishing the course set before them by God. Listen to Paul:

> For I am already being poured out as a drink offering, and the time of my departure is at hand. I have fought the good fight, I have finished the race, I have kept the faith. Finally, there is laid up for me the crown of righteousness, which the Lord, the righteous Judge, will give to me on that Day, and not to me only but also to all who have loved His appearing.
>
> Be diligent to come to me quickly; for Demas has forsaken me, having loved this present world, and has departed for Thessalonica—Crescens for Galatia, Titus for Dalmatia. Only Luke is with me. Get Mark and bring him with you, for he is useful to me for ministry. And Tychicus I have sent to Ephesus. Bring the cloak that I left with Carpus at Troas when you come—and the books, especially the parchments.
>
> 2 Timothy 4:6-12 NKJV

At the end of Paul's life he had every earthly reason to throw in the towel and call it quits. He was locked up in prison under the mad emperor, Nero. All his workers were gone from him except Luke. Demos, one of his own close workers, had forsaken him for the world. He was facing the approach of winter in a damp prison, without his cloak. What could be more discouraging?

Not only was he in need of bodily comfort, but also his Scripture (if he had originally had it) had been taken from him so that he was without its strengthening power. We know this because he asked Timothy to bring the books (scrolls, probably Old Testament books) and parchments (perhaps some of his own inspired letters) when he came to him. Added were, the bad memories he had of his last stay in Ephesus where Alexander the coppersmith did him much evil, and many of the faithful Christians stood with Alexander against Paul. Paul prayed that it might not be held against them but warned Timothy to watch out for the evil Alexander.

Is he discouraged? No, instead he says: "And the Lord shall deliver me from every evil work, and will preserve me unto his heavenly kingdom: to whom be glory for ever and ever" Amen (2 Timothy 4:18). He humbly depended upon the Lord until the end. Finishers like Paul have to lay aside all ambition and self-seeking because this crown rewards those who prevail over the Pride of Life. The letter to Timothy shows examples of winners and losers of this crown.

> . . . for Demas has forsaken me, having loved this present world, and has departed for Thessalonica—Crescens for Galatia, Titus for Dalmatia. Only Luke is with me.
>
> Get Mark and bring him with you, for he is useful to me for ministry. And Tychicus I have sent to Ephesus.
>
> 2 Timothy 4:10-12 NKJV

Looking again at the way Paul grouped his companions in this letter, we can't help but wonder if both Crescens and Titus departed on their own without Paul's blessing, since they are linked with Demos who forsook him. Luke seems to be the dividing line between the two groups. Luke remained faithful, as has Mark who is profitable to the ministry, perhaps implying that the others are not. Then contrast the fact that Tychicus was sent by Paul while the others simply went. Demos and Crescens probably returned home. The Scriptures do not mention where they are from. Titus, however, went on to a new mission field and is credited by history to have been the first to evangelize Dalmatia.

The question is, did God send Titus or did he take it upon himself to go? All other missionary efforts were carried out by a cooperative effort of Paul and his companions under the direction of the Holy Spirit. Did Titus get carried away with his experience and position in the Church and go off seeking the glory of a new campaign? We may never know the answer, but if he did, the "finisher's" crown may be denied him, because in order to finish the course, you have to stay on it. You cannot legitimately finish the race if you jump the track. Another example of someone losing the Crown of Righteousness may be Diotrephes, mentioned in John's third epistle.

> **I wrote to the church, but Diotrephes, who loves to have the preeminence among them, does not receive us. Therefore, if I come, I will call to mind his deeds which he does, prating against us with malicious words. And not content with that, he himself does not receive the brethren, and forbids those who wish to, putting them out of the church. Beloved, do not imitate what is evil, but what is good. He who does good is of God, but he who does evil has not seen God.**
>
> **3 John 9-11AV**

This brother was evidently an elder in the church, because he was using his authority to control others. Can you imagine what audacity it would take to refuse the authority of the Apostle John? One who had been intimately associated with the Lord when he walked upon the earth? Diotrephes loved to feel important. John tells the rest not to follow him, because he that does evil has not seen God. In other words, he goes his own way off the track. Elders are supposed to be examples to others. He was not. He failed to conquer the pride of life.

In conclusion, the three crowns earned for righteous living are for conquering the lust of the flesh, the lust of the eyes and the pride of life. Those believers who earn the Crown of Righteousness will earn all three, because you can't finish the course without doing so.

Adam and Eve faced this same test in the Garden of Eden. Eve saw that the fruit from the tree of knowledge of good and evil was good for food (the lust of the flesh), was pleasant to the eyes (the lust of the eyes), was desired to make one wise (the pride of life). She and Adam both ate it. They failed the test, and sin infected the human race.

Jesus was offered the same test from the Devil. He hungered, so Satan said, "Turn the stones to bread" (lust of the flesh). He showed Jesus the kingdoms of the world and offered them to him if he would worship Satan (the lust of the eyes). Then he took Jesus to the pinnacle of the temple and said throw yourself down and remain unhurt. God will protect you. Be a spectacle in the eyes of the people (the pride of life). Jesus did not succumb but passed the test.

Now it is our turn. Will we overcome the lust of the flesh, the lust of the eyes and the pride of life? Will we at least strive to earn the Incorruptible Crown, the Crown of Life and the Crown of Righteousness?

Crowns for Service

The crowns for service are divided into two categories, with one crown in each. The Crown of Rejoicing rewards those who have had influence in inspiring others to spiritual life and holiness, which involves the faithful use of our motivational gifts, in the sphere in which God places us. The other rewards the Crown of Glory for faithfully shepherding over a local church.

The Crown of Rejoicing

The crown of rejoicing proceeds from a witness. It's a fact that all the truth that we know comes from someone's witness. History consists of happenings recorded by eyewitnesses and by what evidence as is left by former generations and can be researched by scholars. We receive both eye witness reports and scholarly truth through testimony of others. Similarly, we do not search out and discover scientific truth for ourselves either but rely on scientists to experiment and confirm their findings and report them to us. Education itself consists of testimony of people from various fields of endeavor. We accept their findings and hold them to be true by faith in their expertise.

The truths of God are no different. The patriarchs and prophets of the Old Testament laid the foundation of our understanding of God. The Judeo-Christian faith was built upon it. Then Jesus came to earth to finish our understanding by fulfilling the Old Testament's promises. He was his own witness by his life. The Father also bore witness with his voice from heaven. The Holy Spirit confirmed it by acts of power in miracles.

The apostles witnessed his resurrection and gave testimony through the writings of the New Testament. They preached to the world, and the Holy Spirit confirmed their witness with signs and miracles. By their testimony, Christianity spread rapidly throughout the Roman Empire. Each believer had the "good news" of the truth told them by a witness. Since then the whole business of the Church has been to witness to the truth of God's plan for the earth and each person's opportunity to participate in it. The Holy Spirit's confirmation to each believer's own spirit makes him know his salvation has been acquired. He knows that he knows because God talks to him. Because of his "knowing for sure" he becomes a passionate witness to others. Through the centuries, the Holy Spirit imparted more and more understanding to the Church by specially called individuals. These were gifts to the Church known as the fivefold ministry: apostles, prophets, evangelists and pastors and teachers. By these gifts testimony lost by one generation is often restored to another. Thus, the precious truths of God proceed from generation to generation by a witness. The effectiveness of each individual's witness is rewarded by seeing those whose lives they helped change in heaven. This *is* the crown of rejoicing. Paul said to the Thessalonians:

> **For what is our hope, or joy, or crown of rejoicing? Are not even ye in the presence of our Lord Jesus Christ at his coming? For ye are our glory and joy.**
>
> **1 Thessalonians 2:19, 20 AV**

To personally see the lives you have brought into the kingdom or helped grow, crowns your spiritual life. Just as you have satisfaction in the world for work accomplished, so do you have satisfaction in heaven for accomplishing work for God. Paul says that the joy is mutual between worker and receiver.

> Therefore, my beloved, as you have always obeyed, not as in my presence only, but now much more in my absence, work out your own salvation with fear and trembling; for it is God who works in you both to will and to do for His good pleasure.
>
> Do all things without complaining and disputing, that you may become blameless and harmless, children of God without fault in the midst of a crooked and perverse generation, among whom you shine as lights in the world, holding fast the word of life, so that *I may rejoice in the day of Christ* that I have not run in vain or labored in vain.
>
> Yes, and if I am being poured out as a drink offering on the sacrifice and service of your faith, *I am glad and rejoice with you* all. *For the same reason you also be glad and rejoice with me.*
>
> **Philippians 2:12-18 NKJV (Emphasis mine)**

The Philippians were joyful and full of gratitude for the apostle's teaching and encouragement. The apostle was rejoicing in the Philippians' obedience and progress in Christian growth. He was more than willing to sacrifice his life for their improvement. He counted it a joy. But most of all, he rejoiced in the satisfaction that his work accomplished something for God.

Jesus exhorted His disciples as he sent them on a missionary journey:

> "He who receives you receives Me, and he who receives Me receives Him who sent Me. He who receives a prophet in the name of a prophet shall receive a prophet's reward. And he who receives a righteous man in the name of a righteous man shall receive a righteous man's reward. And whoever gives one of these little ones only

> a cup of cold water in the name of a disciple, assuredly, I say to you, he shall by no means lose his reward."
>
> Matthew 10:40-42 NKJV

If the disciples' testimony concerning the kingdom of God being at hand (vs.7) was received, then the hearers would believe the claims of Christ and the truth of God His Father when He addressed them at His appearance on the scene. Thus, the disciples would prepare a people to follow Jesus and witness His death and resurrection. These people would have their faith confirmed and would be the basis of the foundation of the Church on the day of Pentecost. All was built by witnessing to the truth of God and having the witness received by the people.

Then Jesus explains that the same reward comes to the prophet and he who receives him as a prophet. Why? It is the prophet's responsibility to understand the truth from the Spirit of God and proclaim it in a clear manner. It is the hearer's responsibility to recognize the voice of the Holy Spirit in it. Both receive from the Spirit alike.

The same could be said of any of the five-fold ministry callings. The proof of their ministry results in believers being won or edified. The apostle (missionary) rejoices that he has won converts to Christ in a foreign country. The evangelist rejoices to see people saved, healed, and delivered in his home country. The pastor rejoices to see his sheep grow to maturity. The teacher rejoices when those he teaches receive the truth and change their lives accordingly. All rejoice to see the people under their influence grow to the point of influencing others.

In the case of receiving a righteous man, it is a question of integrity. If a man is known to tell the truth and deal fairly in all matters of his life, then his witness for God is likely to be received. He does not have to be especially called to the five-fold ministry to witness to others. He influences them by his words and by his life. He who receives his witness will receive at the very least a conviction of his sins, even if he does not repent. Or he may pursue salvation then both can rejoice in heaven and be each other's crown.

In the case of the disciple i.e. a learner, perhaps a new believer giving a cup of cold water, Jesus says even he will not lose his reward. Why? Because he serves another in the name of Christ and this, too, is a witness and produces joy in the servant and his Lord.

In the parable of the talents (Matthew 25:14-30), Jesus describes the rewarding of faithful servants.

To the servant that had the greatest ability He gave the most negotiating power (money). To the next man He gave a lesser amount. Both of these servants gained the same, 100%. Although their abilities were not equal, their work was the same. But the third man was lazy and self-indulgent. He wasted his time, and at the same time accused the Lord of evil (blaspheming). The two successful servants received the crown of rejoicing. Listen to the Lord's words, "Well done, thou good and faithful servant: thou hast been faithful over a few things, I will make thee ruler over many things: enter thou into *the joy of thy lord.*" Just as Paul could call the Thessalonians his crown of rejoicing, so the Lord rejoices to see us accomplish His works. It makes Him glad. His praise in turn makes us glad. Thus, the crown of rejoicing is a shared crown of joy: the minister, those ministered to and the Lord.

The Crown of Glory

The crown of glory is reserved for elders/pastors who tend the local flock of God's people. Those who attain this office already have a righteous living standard because of the rigorous requirements for this office. Two of Paul's letters state these requirements. They are found in I Timothy 3 and Titus 1.

They are combined into the following list:

1. His life must be above reproach.
2. He must have only one wife.
3. He must be vigilant—alertly discreet—living in an awareness of the circumstances surrounding life.
4. He must be sober (that is, sound in mind and moderate in opinion and passion, having good behavior, not overbearing or quick-tempered.
5. He must be hospitable.
6. He must be able to teach.
7. He must be temperate in regard to wine.
8. He must not be given to physical violence (no striker with fists).
9. He must not be greedy for money.
10. He must not be covetous or envious of other's gain.
11. He must manage his own house well (so that he can manage the Church); therefore, his children must be believers and not have a reputation for being wild and rebellious.
12. He must be a seasoned believer, not a novice, lest he be proud.
13. He must have a good reputation in the world.

We can see from these requirements that one must already be a very righteous man before taking on the added responsibility of overseeing the lives of other Christians. Therefore, it is fitting that a special reward be given for this job.

Unlike the other ministries of prophet, evangelist, or even an apostle, the pastor is charged with taking care of the everyday lives of the church members. The other ministers may come for a season and then end. But the pastor/shepherd deals with his sheep daily. This is often a thankless job as his charges, like sheep, can be unruly and rebellious.

The job of a shepherd is actually threefold. He is an elder in the faith, having attained maturity and wisdom and therefore able to lead others. He is an overseer, a bishop, able to discern problems and correct them; bind their wounds and heal them; and detect any impending dangers. As their shepherd, he feeds them with teaching and nurtures them to maturity.

Peter describes the reward for this work in 1 Peter 5:1-4: NKJV

> **The elders who are among you I exhort, I who am a fellow elder and a witness of the sufferings of Christ, and also a partaker of the glory that will be among you, serving as overseers, not by compulsion but willingly not for dishonest gain but eagerly; nor as being lords over those entrusted to you, but being examples to the flock; and when the Chief Shepherd appears, you will receive the crown of glory that does not fade away.**

Peter declares himself to be an elder, probably because he was currently pastoring a church in Babylon.[11] Then he makes reference to his apostleship when he says

---

[11] Some teachers believe Babylon refers to the city of Rome.

he witnessed Christ's sufferings. And finally he mentions that he partook of the glory, which is future, when he saw Jesus transfigured. These are his credentials for saying what he does about the rewards to follow good pastoring. First, he mentions the three facets of the Pastor's work.

1. Feed the flock, which is teaching them the truths of God.

2. Oversee them (often a time-consuming vocation) sometimes without pay. Warn them of dangers in the world or in their lives personally.

3. Be a leader who is an example, not a tyrant demanding obedience, but patient with the unruly, using gentleness to persuade to righteousness, always holding up the goal of Christ for their lives.

Then he mentions the reward for such faithful service: a crown of glory.

But those truly worthy of this crown of glory should also have already qualified for all the other crowns. No wonder Paul says he that desires the office of an elder (who is also a pastor) desires a good office, because a pastor must have already been willing to add all the other qualities to his faith that Peter had exhorted all believers to add (2 Peter 2-11 NKV).

Peter was an eyewitness to the Lord's glory at the trans-figuration. Here again he could speak with authority. This unforgettable experience made a great impression on Peter, because he mentions it again in his second letter. After exhorting believers to make their calling and election sure by adding righteous living to their faith, he said, "For so an entrance shall be ministered unto you into the everlasting kingdom of our Lord and Savior Jesus Christ." Clearly he speaks of receiving rewards. Jesus delights to reward his people. The crowns are the "well dones," thou good and faithful servants.

The ultimate purpose of God in this world is to dwell with man, and later to train him to rule in His ever expanding (Isaiah 9:7) universe in eternity. That is where He started, with Adam and Eve before sin entered the world. But now the only way a holy God can live with mankind is to save them, then change them into His own likeness so that they can become compatible companions. Then He will have many sons like His Son, Jesus. Revelation 21:3 declares His purpose:

"Behold the tabernacle [dwelling] of God is with men, and he shall dwell with them, and they shall be his people, and God himself shall be with them, and be their God."

Jesus came to fulfill the will of the Father. He did his part. He left us the instructions for our part. Now it is up to us as individuals to submit to God's rule through His Righteousness Laws. Does this standard seem too high? Perhaps, but if we aim at nothing we will hit it every time. The Holy Spirit has come to help us. Let us strive to please him by obedience, showing Blatant Christianity to this world!